The Social Organization of Zen Practice

The Social Organization of Zen Practice

Constructing Transcultural Reality

DAVID L. PRESTON
San Diego State University

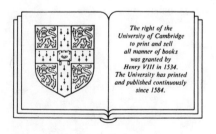

*The right of the
University of Cambridge
to print and sell
all manner of books
was granted by
Henry VIII in 1534.
The University has printed
and published continuously
since 1584.*

CAMBRIDGE UNIVERSITY PRESS

Cambridge

New York   New Rochelle   Melbourne   Sydney

Published by the Press Syndicate of the University of Cambridge
The Pitt Building, Trumpington Street, Cambridge CB2 1RP
32 East 57th Street, New York, NY 10022, USA
10 Stamford Road, Oakleigh, Melbourne 3166, Australia

First published 1988

Printed in the United States of America

Library of Congress Cataloging-in-Publication Data
Preston, David L.

The Social Organization of Zen Practice.

Bibliography: p.

Includes index.

1. Monastic and religious life (Zen Buddhism) –
United States. 2. Zen Buddhism – Social aspects –
United States. I. Title.
BQ9294.4.U6P74   1988   294.3'927   87–23909

British Library Cataloguing in Publication Data
Preston, David L.

The Social Organization of Zen Practice:
Constructing Transcultural Reality.

1. Zen Buddhism
I. Title
294.3'927   BQ9265.4

ISBN 0 521 35000 X

To Jeana and Emilie

Contents

Foreword

How is one to write about Zen Buddhism? It seems, on the face of it, an antidiscursive or even anti-intellectual religion, defying efforts to formulate its doctrine in so many words, or any words at all. It is famous for its putdowns of the intellectual stance, for its revelations through paradox, for its sudden experiences that break through ordinary concepts and perceptions and into the wordlessness of a truer reality. At the same time, its mysticism is antimystical: Zen practice shuns the deep trance states, requires meditation with eyes half open, and has insisted on groundedness in the ordinary world. It is no wonder that most writers on Zen fall back on paradoxes and exhortations, leaving the subject wrapped in an air of mysteriousness – or humor – that for Western sophisticates often seems to border on self-caricature.

The standard authors – Watts, Suzuki, Kapleau – have resorted to the use of paradox in their attempts to preach for an antidoctrinal doctrine. David Preston's account, though, takes a different route, and he comes closer to his goal, perhaps, than most of his illustrious predecessors. It may well be the most informative book yet written about Zen, or any of the Asian meditative religions. The author's approach is not to extol the religion, its therapeutic significance, or its cultural heritage. Instead, he takes us through Zen naturalistically, informing us of the ordinary reality of the experience: the physical setting, the members of the group, the teacher, the routine, the inner experience and its struggles. This review builds up to a wonderful revelation of the meanings of Zen practice. It is, in short, an ethnography of Zen Buddhism, an "insider's report." His account is full of the anthropological detail, the mundane reality of the whole enterprise, that the more uplift-oriented variety of Zen literature leaves aside. Yet Preston manages to use the mundane as a path beyond itself; and I suspect he captures more of the actuality of Zen than the flamboyant writers do.

Preston's report is realistic and unromanticized. We are a long way from the Chan masters of ninth- and tenth-century China, with their blows and shouts awakening their thick-headed disciples. One of the weaknesses of the doctrinal–inspirational version of Zen literature is its anachronism; by focusing on the paradoxical koans and the tales of the great masters, these writers obscure the historical fact that this early, formative phase of Chan occurred long ago. Already when Chan arrived in medieval Japan (becoming Zen), the koans had been collected and turned into a form of student exercise, a discipline to be studied, a series of stages to be passed in a well-ordered monastic career. Although Preston's account is not historical, it gives us a fresher, clearer view of modern, institutionalized Zen, as it actually exists, that makes the more famous accounts look quasi-ideological by comparison.

But Preston does not try to deflate Zen either. His work is not an expose. In fact, it seems to achieve an unbiased expression of a Zen attitude in its very naturalism. Preston may actually have accomplished the writing of a Zen book about Zen, which turns out to be far different from the usual paradoxes and verbal clevernesses about one hand clapping.

Preston neither attacks nor endorses the doctrinal interpretation of Zen. He simply does not use Zen doctrine as his starting point or frame of interpretation; he tells what the Zen organization and its activities are like, from his own observation and experience and from interviews, gradually building up to a sophisticated evocation and analysis of meditation and its meanings. This naturalistic approach permits Preston to conclude his work with an intellectual analysis, precisely on the issue of nonverbalizable experiences. I think his presentation is successful, because, as a sociologist, he takes intellectual analysis simply as another natural activity. As a result, we learn more about Zen than we do from the more mystical and self-conscious accounts of it.

Preston's book has other merits as well, both as sociology of religion and as an advance in microsociological theory. As such, I believe it carries significance not only for social scientists but also for philosophers and theologians. Let me attempt to suggest where this significance lies.

As sociology of religion. One of Preston's underlying themes is to expand our general understanding of the social nature of religion. Prevailing approaches in the sociology of religion are variants of social or psychological reductionism. Such analyses see religion as merely another instance of socialization – of joining a social movement, of community pressures, or of compensation for psychological stresses. Although these aspects of socialization may exist, Preston seeks to identify the distinctively *religious* element in its practices. In what way does religion escape from being merely another secular process? Preston's strategy, then, is to focus on how religious practices construct a special field of experience, one that is aimed at overcoming normal socially induced modes of perception and that is, so to speak, layered over them to provide an emergent level of reality. By the later chapters of the book, the evidence compiled by Preston reveals the methods by which socially grounded processes transcend themselves, with the creation or emergence of a transcultural level of reality. Religious practice, at its most profound, is intrinsically multileveled; Preston spells out the kinds of subjective, objective, and fundamental/intuitive meanings that constitute the reality of Zen. This approach gets closer to "giving religion its due" than most other efforts from the social sciences. Preston gives us an understanding of what is distinctive about religious reality, without ceasing to be a sociologist. The religious and social levels are not antithetical. However mundane the social level may appear, it is the base, and a self-transforming one, from which transcendental religious experience emerges. Preston's formulation should be of challenging interest to students of modern theology as well.

As sociological theory. Preston's work is based on the theories of social phenomenology and ethnomethodology, in combination with his own blend of the ideas of Bourdieu and Goffman and my own theory of rituals and emotional energy in everyday life. Let us briefly review some of the salient points of these theories.

Garfinkel's ethnomethodology is a radical social constructionism. Reality is not given but emerges from practices of reasoning in everyday life, which draws on the stock of "commonsense" knowledge in people's culture. Garfinkel gives a somewhat paradoxical tone to his social phenomenology by stressing the properties of indexicality and reflexivity. The theory of indexicality suggests that everything is embedded in a surrouding context that must be taken for granted in order to know what it is. If one tries to state explicity the assumed background, this leads to a still further context that is taken for granted, and so on. To avoid this infinite regress people use the procedures of commonsense reasoning. According to the theory of reflexivity, we live in a world of particular situations, although we use general concepts to interpret them; however, these general concepts are never directly seen but only illustrated by alleged examples of them. There is no escape from this circular relationship.

Garfinkel claims that the procedures by which people account for circumstances or events represent the way social reality was constructed in the first place. The ordinariness of the world is not given but is socially produced, although people censor their awareness of having done this cognitive work. Reflexivity is hidden by "the natural attitude." People assume that meanings will eventually emerge and do not insist that everything be meaningful the moment they experience it. Only when something happens to disturb their sense of the normal flow of action do they examine social reality; usually they offer "accounts" that quickly restore the sense of normality. The world is held together not because people agree on a single reality but because they refrain from questioning reality.

One might infer that Garfinkel's ethnomethodology is a bit like a sociological version of Zen. Here is a world that will not bear too much examination. Things are what they are, but only as long as we do not press very hard on them; when we do, meaning fades away as our explicit reasoning chases them into an infinite regress. A major difference between Garfinkel's concepts and Zen, though, is that whereas Zen puts its practitioners through long training to achieve this attitude toward reality, Garfinkel proposes that everyone already has such an attitude: It is the height of the mundane, the essence of commonsense practical reasoning. Ethnomethodology, in short, has no place for Preston's culminating idea of "transcultural reality," which Zen uncovers. The phenomenological camp tends toward relativism and the "local production" of infinite varieties of knowledge, none of which transcends its immediate circumstances. But Preston goes beyond Garfinkel's version of philosophical paradoxes and tries to understand the process of social interpretation and meaning construction in a naturalistic way, as an objective feature of the world. Religious reality, in Zen, is not merely local and subjective; it is transcendent and objective, and founded in natural, social processes that themselves have an objective contour that may be sociologically described.

Preston, in other words, is concerned with the social construction of religious reality. While sensitive to the procedures of everyday reasoning documented by the ethnomethodologists, he does not simply accept their relativism but seeks methods by which objective realities may themselves be naturalistically produced. There is theoretical precedent for this approach in the Durkheimian tradition, especially as developed by Goffman (whose ideas in turn I have exploited still further). In this view, subjective realities are collective products; but their base has an objective reality, because it is the ritualized interaction of real human bodies coming together in time and space that produces the symbols that represent collective experience. In Durkheim's fundamental model, rituals are interactions in which participants stereotype their actions; become mutually aware of a common focus of attention, and hence implicitly of the overriding presence of the group; and propagate a common emotion or mood. In this way participants produce symbolic, "sacred objects," charged up with a moral force because they act as reminders of a group-created common reality.

Durkheim himself favored the hypothesis that a group's symbols directly reflect the physical structure of the group, a hypothesis that has had to be abandoned for lack of evidence. Durkheim's primary interest was in moral realities, sentiments of solidarity within the group; on this level, his dictum that the religion symbolizes the constraints of membership in society is defensible. But it neglects the transcendental aspect of religion, its capacity (which emerges only in rather cosmopolitan religions) to point not only beyond the existing society but even beyond the cosmos. This is the kind of "transcultural reality" at which Zen is pointed. And indeed, a sociological justification for seeing such a formulation of transcultural reality as an emergent *social* property comes from a later development of the Durkheimian tradition, the work of Erving Goffman.

Goffman's *frame analysis* avoids the extremes of sheer physical objectivity and subjective relativism by using a set of levels building on one another. Human beings orient first to the "primary frameworks" of the physical world and human bodies within it; they then can construct *transformations,* which change the meaning of activity into make-believe, contests, ceremonials, deceptions, and other reformulations. Transformations can be built on transformations, resulting in high levels of complexity. The framing continuum is in principle open-ended at the "upper" end, but grounded in an objective physical world at the "bottom." Thus, rituals can become increasingly reflexive, self-referential, and sophisticated; the realities that they construct – or reveal – are precisely this formative, multileveled nature of the human world itself.

Preston makes a creative extension of the theory of interaction rituals, taking it onto new grounds and achieving new results. In effect, he is proposing that Zen meditation is itself a type of ritual, especially focused back upon itself. At the "bottom" end, it is grounded in the human body. Here Preston connects with the ethnomethodology on embodied practices developed by David Sudnow (another of Goffman's former pupils). Preston's Chapter VII, "Doing Zen Meditation," draws a striking parallel to Sudnow's analysis of the experience of learning to play jazz piano. In both cases, one learns to let the body take over from the mind; yet through this "letting go," the mind goes not downward but upward, toward a higher level of communication or of consciousness.

Apart from the special application to religious practices and meanings, Preston's work has another benefit that theoretical sociologists should ponder. It happens that Zen is a particularly good site on which to explore the nature of reflexive subjectivity, of consciousness and the unconscious, of emotion and cognition, and their multiple levels of meaning. The transcultural reality that Preston – and Zen – reveals is the self-constructing nature of the human mind itself.

RANDALL COLLINS
University of California, Riverside

Preface

To write about Zen is a challenging task. Those who practice Zen or who are sympathetic to it for aesthetic reasons often find words inadequate to describe the richness and vitality of the realm. Those more critically disposed find any seeming reluctance on the part of the writer to dissect the Zen setting as dispassionately as any other to be annoying and even perhaps to reveal an overabundance of misplaced respect – a suspicion that can lead to rejection of the value of the writing as a whole.

This book tries to please both groups. In other words, I have tried to express some features of members' (including the writer's) experience in the Zen setting, and the insights glimpsed therein, in the language of sociology. This approach entails some compromises, although not destructive ones. In their classical writings, the practitioners of the major meditative forms have often expressed their experience in terms that are recognizably psychological and have attempted, in the most general sense, to make some contribution to the understanding of the mind and its operation. In contrast, the present study tries to see Zen practice in terms that take seriously the collective (i.e., social) processes of forming and reforming our ways of thinking, feeling, and acting.

My position is that meditative practices such as those found in the Zen setting directly affect the social and psychological processes that are the basis of all shared experiences of reality. This view is not new. Its psychological equivalent can be found in classic texts on meditation and in contemporary psychological literature. This approach, however, has not been used to examine meditative practices sociologically, that is, with the emphasis not on individual but on group processes that both support meditative activity and produce agreement on its meaning. I hope to contribute to the understanding of how one comes to be a member of a Zen group and similar groups using meditative practices, and to show the important differences between such groups and those lacking these practices. One result of this analysis will be an appreciation of the inadequacy of received notions in social theory of what is involved in socialization – the process of becoming a member of any group.

Further, the descriptions and analyses presented in this study suggest not only that the processes of joining a religious group using meditative practices are different, but that what is joined itself is qualitatively different from what is normally taken as mundane reality in all its myriad local forms. I hope to illustrate that the claims made by transpersonal psychologists studying features of human experience (religious experience, for example) that go beyond typical notions of personality and ego have a sociological dimension as well. I am, then, exploring possibilities suggested by Ken Wilber's (1983) advice to identify the fundamental psychosocial relationships constitutive of the contemplative realms.

It cannot be emphasized enough that Zen is not an intellectual enterprise and the account of it found in this study is not at all that suggested by the teachings of Zen (although it is not entirely incompatible with these teachings). The goals and practices of Zen are soteriological, whereas those of sociology are both different and more limited. This does not prevent Zen practitioners from recognizing an adequate sociological account of their practice. Those members of the groups studied who have read all or parts of this manuscript have found it to be a credible description of their experience in general. I suspect that it will be found generally adequate for Zen groups in America.

I readily admit that I am no expert on Buddhism and thus cannot even begin to make my view of Zen conform to some orthodox standard, whatever that might mean in a Zen context. The view of Zen Buddhism found in this work is largely that of the writer, which has been shaped by doing Zen practice and by interacting with the teachers and, especially, the members of the groups studied. American Zen practitioners are not always well informed on Buddhism beyond some acquaintance with its most basic teachings. This lack of knowledge is not a fault for our purposes; it simply constitutes part of the context in which Zen exists in America. Because Zen emphasizes "a special transmission outside the Scriptures" (Suzuki, 1956, 9) that is based largely on meditative practices, the neglect by some practitioners of textual training is entirely understandable.

Chapter I gives a statement of the main concerns of the study, its purposes, and the methods used to produce this account. The next three chapters describe the Zen experience. In Chapter II, I discuss the social characteristics of members as well as the formal organization of one center and its physical layout. Chapter III introduces a Zen teacher and outlines some forms of his interaction with students. The issue of authority is raised in this chapter but deferred until after meditation is discussed as a reality-building process. Chapter IV then considers how and what one learns in a new-practitioner's workshop and discusses some varieties of Zen practice. These descriptive chapters provide the basis for the theoretical discussions that follow. Chapter V presents a somewhat modified symbolic interactionist view of Zen practice and introduces the issues that are pursued in the next four chapters. Chapter VI develops an alternative to the constructionist perspective on conversion by treating meditation as a social phenomenon. Chapter VII gives an example of how Zen experience is accomplished around the problems of pain and of actively trying to "do" meditation. Elements of the social organization of Zen practice are also outlined. Chapter VIII examines ritual meditative practice and its consequences. Periods of intensive practice (*sesshin*) are examined in terms of how they contribute to the attenuation of old habits and practices of reality construction and the development of alternative reality-construction practices. Chapter IX considers three different meanings of Zen practice and how they are produced by different practitioners using different practices. Finally, in Chapter X I make some observations of a general nature about the relevance of this study for sociology.

Without the encouragement and support of many people this work would not have been completed. In its early stages, the efforts of Professor Leonard Pinto of the University of Colorado, Boulder, were especially encouraging. Later, Richard Boyle gave generously of his time to read various drafts of my work and allowed me to use his extensive unpublished manuscript on the structure of mystical teachings.

My student and friend Gary Novak provided the kind of critical feedback, personal support, and gentle instruction that is a model of cheerful collegiality.

My colleagues in the sociology department at San Diego State University helped out in various ways from copyediting to providing substantive criticisms. Their patient encouragement over the years is appreciated.

Professor Robert Ellwood of the University of Southern California and Professor Bennett Berger of the University of California at San Diego read the entire manuscript and made helpful and sometimes quite critical suggestions for improvement.

Professor Randall Collins of the University of California at Riverside read the manuscript carefully and insightfully, and his review resulted in a significantly improved revision. His scholarship, attention to subtleties of argument, and openness to sociological explorations that might seem marginal to his interests are greatly appreciated.

My greatest debt intellectually is to those whose names appear recurrently in the list of references. They are my most recent teachers in sociology. The writings of Ken Wilber, whom I have never met, could not have been more helpful. His work promises to be the basis for a whole new direction in the study of religion. The writings of Herbert Fingarette encouraged me to undertake the study of a topic that is marginal to mainstream sociology and showed me how it could be done. I have learned much from the work of Katsuki Sekida, Phillip Kapleau, and Joseph Damrell, and all deserve special thanks. On rereading their work, I often realize that much of what I had been thinking of as my own ideas I actually learned from them.

I would like to express special thanks to my teacher Hakuyu Taizan Maezumi-roshi, the abbot of the Zen Center of Los Angeles. His support of my research made the interviewing of staff and other members of the Los Angeles Center possible at a very busy time.

I would like to thank the members and teachers in both Los Angeles and San Diego who agreed to be interviewed for this study. Charlotte Joko Beck, the teacher in residence in San Diego, and Elizabeth Yuin Hamilton deserve special mention in this regard.

Grateful acknowledgment is made for permission to reprint the following published materials: "Becoming a Zen Practitioner" by David L. Preston, from *Sociological Analysis* 1981, 42, 1, reprinted by permission of the journal *Sociological Analysis;* and "Meditative Ritual Practice and Spiritual Conversion-Commitment: Theoretical Implications Based on the Case of Zen" by David L. Preston, from *Sociological Analysis* 1982, 43, 3, reprinted in part by permission of the journal *Sociological Analysis.*

The photographs in this study are used with the permission of the Zen Center of Los Angeles. I am especially grateful to have had access to the excellent photo archives of this center, whose staff more than once took time from very demanding schedules to aid my research.

Technical support was provided at important intervals by Professor Harry King of San Diego State University and the staff of the sociology department, namely, Lilian Marcus and Beth Snyder.

I am especially appreciative of the diligent work and the skills of the staff at the New York branch of Cambridge University Press, especially acquisitions editor David Emblidge, who first saw the value of the project.

Finally I would like to acknowledge the loving support given by my wife, Jeana, who, despite the demands of her own career, in her own words, "made the tuna sandwiches."

CHAPTER I

A Sociological View of Zen

What makes Zen practice sociologically interesting? Although this entire book attempts to answer this question, a few points can be stated simply at the outset. First, Zen tends to be very different from what we often take as typical religious activity in the United States and Europe. Some of those who practice Zen, for example, do not even consider it a religion. It has no notion of a supernatural being and no conflict with science. In fact, Zen attracts many scientists and persons with advanced degrees. Second, like a variety of Eastern religious forms, Zen involves meditative practices and an explicit notion of training that uses such practices. A close examination of these practices necessitates a reconsideration of standard social scientific notions of what happens in "religious" settings. Third, Goffman (1974) recommends just this sort of study.

The first object of social analysis ought, I think to be ordinary, actual behavior – its structure and its organization. However, the student, as well as his subjects, tends to take the framework of everyday life for granted; he remains unaware of what guides him and them. Comparative analysis of realms of being provides one way to disrupt this unselfconsciousness. *Realms of being other than the ordinary provide natural experiments in which a property of ordinary activity is displayed or contrasted in a clarified and clarifying way.* The design in accordance with which everyday experience is put together can be seen as a special variation on general themes, as ways of doing things that can be done in other ways. (Goffman, 1974, 564; emphasis added)

Although this volume is clearly a study of a religious topic, its relevance is not limited to just religious issues or confined to religious interests. What are "strictly" religious issues? If they can be categorized at all, such issues would perhaps include those that concern trends in the growth or demise of various churches or denominations, or the problems of clergy in particular organized settings. Other examples of strictly religious issues

1

might be proposed, but these examples serve to show what this study is not directly concerned with, namely, religion as it is ordinarily conceived of in America. Both commonsense and "enlightened" intellectual opinion often know what religion is. And what they know is that it is either for them or not for them, something to be valued or devalued, respected or disrespected. From the negative side of this certainty, there is little one can read or, in fact, imagine that would be interesting about religion. Previously, I had refused to label the material of this study as "religious" simply because it was too interesting to be so. Now, however, I am willing to call it religious but urge the reader to be cautious before assuming that the meaning of this word is clear. I will offer my own definition early in the study; however, we should remember that definitions often cannot address broader commitments and interests that have nonconceptual roots. The concerns and interests of this study go beyond an analysis of religion as the word is often used. They reflect directly on both personal growth and broader issues in social theory.

Approaching the Study of Religion

One of the most important studies of the psycho-social-spiritual boundary is that by Fingarette, who suggests the "evils" to be avoided in such a study.

I have in mind here two special evils. One consists in psychologizing the spiritual life ("reducing" it to psychology with nothing left over). The other evil consists in mistaking widespread, popular perversions of the spiritual life for the real thing, thus often providing incisive analyses of something which is familiar though incorrectly labeled. (Fingarette, 1963, 6)

As Bellah has pointed out, even Durkheim's work on religion can be faulted as being reductionistic in that he accounts for religion entirely in terms of the social world. An example of this error is also found in Freud's *Future of an Illusion;* more recent examples are available as well, including much of the work done on "cults" following the Jonestown incident and, in my opinion, Lasch's *The Culture of Narcissism.* As an alternative, Fingarette recommends finding authentic forms of spiritual expression and studying them. Surprisingly, this approach is rarely used by social scientists.

Those who approach spirituality under the guise of religious conversion typically assume that one who joins a religious group does so from a position of weakness (Heirich, 1977). Stress or other difficulties lead one to seek a personal transformation, so that one becomes willing to do what a normal, healthy person would not do – that is, accept a whole new set of values and beliefs in order to reduce the dissonance or to overcome the crisis in which one finds oneself. This study does not make such an assumption: If new members are often dissatisfied with their lives and have a willingness to try something new, the *consequences* of such a willingness to change cannot be dismissed. Certainly one must be willing to enter a religious practice with a general attitude of receptivity, but this does not allow us to ignore what then happens or to define all cases, as is often done, as regression, escape, or retreat into magic or mythic modalities of collective being.

Another common assumption of many sociologists who study religion is that there is nothing special about religious socialization (Berger & Luckmann, 1966; McGuire, 1981). Supposedly a candidate for membership in any group faces the same problems and the same processes in learning the group's ways. Two objections can be made to this assumption and the theories based on it. First, the notion of socialization itself is so general as to disguise what we want to examine in more detail – namely, the particular practices and activities that members use in particular situations to produce appropriate behavior and make sense of their circumstances. Second, although some religious settings can be seen as nearly identical to nonreligious settings, those examined in this study are clearly not so. In fact, what we observe in the Zen setting is to some degree a case of desocialization, unlearning rather than relearning.

To appreciate the first objection that the use of the term "socialization" needs to be used very carefully, let us look at some basic assumptions about the social actor and how socialization occurs according to the two major ways of doing sociological research, what Wilson (1970) calls the "normative" and "interpretive" paradigms.

In the normative approach social interaction is seen as governed by rules. One learns a role, which is a set of rules and expectations, and behavior is accounted for by locating the actor in a structure of these shared expectations. Since all members of a social setting tend to agree on what is happening and what things mean because they are socialized into the same roles and norms, they can interact in an orderly fashion. A second feature of this approach is the demand that explanation be a deductive process. As in the natural sciences, facts are explained by deducing them logically from theory. The sociologist is seen to have a privileged position from which to observe and understand the processes and structures of the social world.

The major alternative to this normative approach – the interpretive view – is made up of various schools of thought and research (phenomenological sociologies and symbolic interaction to mention just two) that share a few common assumptions. The actor, not the rule, governs interaction. The actor is a working participant in the processes of making sense of the world by interacting with others. One does not just "release" behavior under certain structural conditions (as in the view of the normative perspective), but one negotiates an agreement on what seems appropriate and real in a particular situation. Further, because the world as seen through the eyes of particular social actors is given such importance, it becomes the relevant basis for understanding social activity. The normative notion that actors somehow lead their lives by the tenets of social theory without really knowing it is recognized as inadequate. To the extent that social theory is not based on actors' realities and on the practices that actors use to devise a common reality, it is off the mark.

What happens, then, in the process of becoming a member of a group – that is, in the process of socialization – is quite different according to each of these viewpoints.[1] The current study closely follows the members' experience and attempts to build an account of Zen practice that is informed by such experience. An explicit effort is made to follow the interpretive approach to the process of becoming a member, although our description and analysis goes beyond that suggested by this approach. Before turning to the argument that socialization in the Zen setting is considerably different from other settings, one last assumption that bears on this argument should be considered. Social scientific studies of religious or ideological groups commonly make the assumption that the truth claims of such groups must be criticized and shown to be of less value than the claims of social science. Coulter (1979) refers to this as the "ironic attitude" of these studies – ironic because social scientists assume that what they are doing to the objects of their studies cannot be done to their own perspectives and truth claims.

The contemporary Mannheimian sociology of knowledge and belief has perpetuated, with sociology, this constitution of members' beliefs-about-society (or about certain of its features) as *essentially competing sociological theories* rather than as integral parts of the societies within which they are held. . . . Lay sociological beliefs are investigated for their possible *truth value,* rather than as empirical features of a society to be analyzed, along with other beliefs, in terms of their socially organized properties. (Coulter, 1979, 165; emphasis altered)

If we take Coulter's advice, questions must be asked about how people come to experience a common reality in a particular form, what do they do to produce this experience, and how do they come to agree on its meaning? The focus is on how a particular reality is constituted, produced, and shared rather than on criticizing its alleged shortcoming vis à vis a scientific viewpoint.

This perspective urged by Coulter stops short of the relativism typical of many sociological studies. He believes his view is privileged – namely, a view that sees how all realities are produced or what they all have in common. Ethnomethodology and phenomenological sociologies tend to argue in favor of an approach to the study of social aspects that does not stop just with ethnography or with understanding the meanings that members of a group share. They go beyond this to the study of the presuppositions and practices used by members of a group to produce a sense of shared reality. These practices and presuppositions are not usually known to members (even as they use them) but rather are prior to, and constitutive of, the meanings with which the typical ethnography deals. This study is informed by this approach.

How can the practice of Zen be studied as a social phenomenon? This study does so by asking the question, "How is a sense of shared reality produced among those doing Zen practice?" The answer, which is based on a variety of sociological theorists, is that the Zen setting is socially organized in such a way as to facilitate the experience of an alternative way of being, or a shared sense of reality. Of course, this claim could be made about any group – namely, that the reality that members share is the product of particular socially organized presuppositions, practices, and interactions. The possibility that the Zen and other similar settings have special features in this regard will be addressed shortly.

Schutz (1967) has argued that the reality commonly experienced in everyday life is but one of a wide variety of realities (or provinces of meaning). We also encounter the realities of fantasy, scientific theorizing, dreaming, and religious experience, for example. Each of these realities is constituted by what Schutz calls its cognitive style or the set of presuppositions and modes of activity that constitute it. Each is equally real and internally consistent, but commonsense reality is considered predominant because we must return to it to communicate with one another. In this view, religious experience is a reality that is linked to specific cognitive features seen to help produce the experience in consciousness. These features, then, become some of the elements for a sociological study of how the practice of Zen is constituted.

Schutz's theories can be improved upon and expanded by reference to the work of ethnomethodologists. Particular practices used by members are examined and rules outlined for understanding how one makes a shared sense of reality out of the flow of everyday life. For most who work from this perspective, language plays the key role in shaping social reality. This emphasis on language and talk can lead to difficulties, however, when applied to a Zen setting. Talk is deemphasized in Zen practice, and nonverbal training of the body (and mind) is made prominent. A study of how Zen reality is constituted, then, must focus closely on this process of body (and mind) training and its experience on the part of the practitioner. This focus parallels the work of some sociologists, even if it is a less well followed path.

Social meanings are continuously created and recreated through the situated praxis which presupposes, preserves, and uses those meanings. Thus, "table" is a gloss for the cognitive, practical, and interactional work through which "table" is enacted. . . . From this point of view, the table is created and sustained by virtue of what is done to, with, or about it. (Pollner, 1979, 249)

One could extrapolate then from Pollner: "Zen" is a gloss for the cognitive, practical, and interactional work through which "Zen" is enacted. Like any other social phenomenon, it is defined by the activities that accomplish it. Seen in this light, Zen practice is a set of activities, attitudes, and rituals that are organized by the notion of enlightenment into a more or less coherent, if flexible, whole. The practice includes sitting meditation, chanting, interviews with a teacher, hearing talks by a teacher, as well as the activities and work assignments of *sesshin*. It can include any and all the activities of life – eating, walking, and working – depending upon one's commitment to maintaining a meditative stance in these various activities.

The most challenging problem in doing a sociological study of Zen (and similar phenomena) is indicated by the fact that Zen itself claims to be uncommunicable in words.[2] Many stories are told about this difficulty. A young student or an official asks a Zen teacher for some explanation and the teacher responds with a seemingly nonsensical gesture or statement. For example:

Whenever he was asked about Zen, Master Gutei simply stuck up one finger. He had a boy attendant whom a visitor asked, "What kind of teaching does your master give?" The boy held up one finger, too. Hearing of this, Gutei cut off the boy's finger with a knife. As the boy ran away screaming with pain, Gutei stuck up one finger. The boy was suddenly enlightened. (Yamada, 1979, 25)

What are we to make of this? According to Wilber (1983, 133), all transrational forms of religion share this difficulty of expressing the reality there encountered in mental-egoic (rational) terms: "For spiritual knowledge itself is not symbolic; it involves direct, nonmediated, trans-symbolic intuition of and identity with spirit."

This would seem to limit severely an approach to Zen as a socially mediated, reflexively organized phenomenon. But this limitation is not as severe as it appears at first sight. I do not argue that Zen is nothing but socially shared meanings. Rather, an account is presented of how Zen practices contribute to the attenuation of the reality-building practices of everyday life; the facilitation of an alternative set of reality-producing activities typical of the transrational realm; and the production of a sense of shared reality among members.

In doing this I am constantly aware, both theoretically and experientially, of the problem of reducing spirituality to social determinants. Thus no claim is made that spiritual knowledge is socially organized in the sense that it is symbolically mediated (although this argument is indeed often made by others). Instead I will argue that the practices facilitating such knowledge are socially organized and, further, that the consequences of such knowledge are observable in social action, even if they cannot be expressed in normal language. This conception of Zen as a sociological phenomenon, then, clearly goes only part way in dealing with the phenomenon in its richness. Focusing in this fashion on the constitutive processes and the work members do to accomplish this reality at best just approaches the limit beyond which such "working" and "doing" cannot be performed. According to the experts, true spiritual knowledge can exist only where there is "surrender" (Wolff, 1976), "non-doing" (Benoit, 1955), or an attitude of active passivity.

Admittedly there are a variety of religious forms that gain access to and express this knowledge somewhat differently. One contemporary Zen teacher writes:

Zen Buddhism does not pervade the cosmos. It presents essential nature – universal mind – but it does so as a particular teaching. Confusing the specific teaching with its vast and undifferentiated subject is a trap that has caught several tigers. (Aitken, 1978, 17)

Put simply (for this issue is considered in greater detail in Chapters VII, VIII, and IX), for the purposes of this study Zen is seen as a reality that is socially organized to the degree that it is learned and shared, and study of these socially organized practices can reveal how people collectively produce and come to agree on the reality of the Zen experience. This involves examination of practices and assumptions, both formal and informal, with an interest in learning something about how this form of reality is encouraged, facilitated, and expressed.

The emphasis put on experience and training of the bodymind in a Zen setting is such that efforts to focus on them involve a close examination of the interactions and experience of members. My primary concern is with learning how members come to share common experiences and meanings in this rather esoteric setting, and how particular practices figure into this process of personal transformation and membership acquisition. I will attempt to show how the group's practices especially, but also their beliefs to a lesser degree, contribute to the realization of a particular way of being human that is rather ambiguously referred to as "Zen."

A method – a way of doing the study, of actually becoming familiar with and documenting a group's particular way of life and its meaning to them – still remains to be considered.

On Going Native

A basic prescription for students who use a participant–observer method of studying a particular group is: Be careful not to "go native" (Bittner 1973). The disciplined observer has a privileged position from which to study social processes only as long as a fine line is walked between what has been called the "absolutist stance" on the one hand and the "natural stance" on the other. The former is that typically taken by the scientific observer of the social world and involves methods and logics that we have briefly outlined under the heading of the "normative" paradigm. This stance involves explaining social behavior in terms that are not real for the persons doing the behaving. The scientist assumes a special view that the person in the street does not have and, thus, is supposedly in a better position from which to account for social forms. The natural stance is, simply put, the viewpoint of the actor, the person being studied. The danger with getting too close to this stance is that the participant–observer ceases to "see" the social processes under study but comes to experience them as familiar. One must, according to this advice, remain outside this experience of the world as natural. The desirable study comes when "the retention of an unbiased interest in *things as they actually present themselves* to the perceiving subjects" is maintained (Bittner, 1973, 122).

This advice is sound, especially given the goals of a phenomenological sociology, one of which is to become and remain aware of the role of presuppositions in constituting shared experience. However, in the experience of the present writer, who was a member first and only later developed the desire to report on the setting sociologically, this advice came too late. So what can be said to legitimate the de facto stance from which the present study was undertaken?

First, there is the issue of what it means to be a member of the group studied. Actually anyone who wants to can be a member and will be considered such almost directly on beginning the practice (and paying the dues). However, this relative notion of membership has nothing to do with the actual accomplishment in Zen practice that is a much more interesting measure of membership. This second notion is similar to the process of, say, learning to do jazz improvisation, where one has abundant evidence of the validity or shortcomings of one's claim to membership among jazz musicians. It is one thing to want to be a member and even to think that one is so; it is another entirely to be able to accomplish the skilled activities in which true membership resides. In the Zen setting, for the present writer, it was not as easy to go native as one might imagine. Let us pursue this notion.

Because beliefs and claims to truth in the form of propositional knowl-edge are such a small part of doing Zen practice, these early, easily as-

A han (wooden sound piece) with rope and striker. The rhythmic strikings of wood on wood is a common sound during *sesshin*. A sign for the front door of the zendo hangs unused in the background.

similable features that usually mark membership in a group are not relevant. The new practitioners are presented with a situation in which they are expected to do meditation and other rituals and discouraged at the same time from talking about "Zen." Highly abstract questions that do not have to do with the actual practice are labeled "philosophic" and considered inappropriate and distracting. Certainly a few theoretical statements are made about the goals of doing Zen practice, the nature of the self and so on, but these are so abbreviated as to be not very helpful in making sense of things.

Practically, however, one comes to use theoretical terms like *samadhi* (concentration) and *makyo* (intense feelings or hallucinations) to see and locate one's experience and share it with others (Preston 1981; also see Chapter V below). This seems to fit the definition of going native – that is, accounting for experience in terms used by members. But using such terms is not merely a matter of reflexively organizing experience to find such "objects" and "events" in one's environment. What these terms are based on is the activity of meditation and the states of consciousness associated with it. Although there are some unique features to Zen members' experience that can be accounted for in terms of their reflexive use of terms learned in the Zen setting, much of what meditators encounter is similar to meditative experience in other settings as well.

Meditation is not an activity or practice unique to any one group and is, in fact, a practice widely shared by the esoteric forms of the major world religions. Of course particular forms of meditation differ from group to group but there is a core of demands and experiences that are common to all (Carrington, 1977; Goleman, 1977; Maliszewski, Twemlow, Brown, & Engler, 1981; Shapiro, 1980; Wilber, 1980). This study takes the position that the practice of meditation can be done without going native to any particular group.

Further, using recent research as well as classic texts (cf. Brown, 1977; Shapiro, 1980), the argument is made that the sorts of experiences encountered during meditation are such that they cannot be dealt with simply as features of a particular group's "local knowledge." Certainly some experiences are, but I will argue (as others have done) that the process of meditation is a form of phenomenological reduction (Sekida, 1975), a looking at rather than through the normal processes of reality construction (Brown 1977). Thus the process of learning to meditate in a Zen setting cannot be treated simply as accepting a new set of typifications (Berger & Luckmann, 1966; Schutz, 1967) or cognitive presuppositions and practices that then are constitutive of the Zen member's experience.

The reason it is not so easy to go native, then, is that one needs to realize some accomplishment in meditation before one can actually experience Zen membership beyond some minimal and quite formal level. The interaction between the Zen context that supports such meditative practice and the actual skill in doing meditation is a close and subtle one, but one needs to be careful not to find membership too quickly where little if any exists. Meditation is addressed at greater length in Chapters V, VI, VII, and VIII.

Another way of legitimating the stance of this study is to show that it does, in fact, have virtues. The way in which parts of this study were done resembles the method used in Sudnow's important study of becoming a jazz pianist (1978). Sudnow, a student of Garfinkel, shares concerns that are often rather ambiguously labeled as those of ethnomethodology, and his goals and methods in this close study of embodied practice are a fine exemplar for an examination of Zen practice. What features are useful for the purposes of the present study? First, one enters into the activity rather than remains outside – that is, the student becomes the phenomenon and studies his or her own experience; second, description, not explanation, is the goal; third, description is done "from the viewpoint of the actor not via introspective consciousness but via examination of concrete problems posed by the task of sustaining an orwderly activity"; and fourth, "to define jazz (as to define any phenomenon of human action) is to describe the body's ways" (Sudnow, 1978, xiii, 146).

This concern with the body and of not holding back from participation in (and, in fact, becoming) the phenomenon is shared by Wolff (1976) as well. Although Wolff's position is certainly different in interesting ways from Sudnow's, his views also provide support and encouragement for the stance taken by the present study. Discussion of his position, especially as it bears on Zen Buddhism, is taken up in Chapters III and VI.

Parts of the following study use a method similar to Sudnow's, and parts use other methods. Analyses are pursued that would not be done by either just the member or just the participant–observer. The combination of member and sociologist gives a unique perspective that, even if not preferred, provides the opportunity for insight and observations that are often interesting to both the member and the sociologist.

The following study will show that what occurs in this setting is considerably different from what studies usually find in religious settings – usually, but not always. As has been indicated previously, the interpretive viewpoint is more fit to study Zen settings and the form of reality shared therein than is a normative viewpoint, because the former stance focuses on the coming-into-being of shared reality and the work the members do in this process. As Pollner has noted:

Were Mead to repent [sic] Durkheim's rule [treat social facts as things], he might write "consider social facts as -ings."

To attend to the -ing of things involves a radical modification of the attitude of everyday life, for it requires attending to the processes of constitution in lieu of the product thus constituted. In attending to the -ing of things one focuses on the course of activity – the form of life – which presupposes, preserves, and thereby produces the particular "thing." The analysis of -ing often requires an archaeological perspective, *for there are many levels – physiological, experiential, praxiological, and cognitive – through which social objects are created and sustained.* (Pollner, 1979, 253; emphasis added)

This quotation could almost serve as an epigraph for the present study, which does, in fact, move through various levels in its description and analysis of Zen practice. Although this may well create some "mischief," in that metatheoretical understanding, theories of conduct, and methods used are more syncretic than entirely consistent (Gergen, 1982), this approach, for better or worse, is one of the givens of this study.

Sudnow wrote his account of becoming a jazz improvising pianist from the perspective of a person who was ultimately a competent member of such a group, not merely an apprentice. This achievement allowed him the insights that he notes as major turning points or qualitative breaks in technique and experience. It is clear that in order to use this particular method of becoming the phenomenon, the degree of one's accomplishment in doing or being the phenomenon is crucial to one's ability to report it. This fact raises the question of the present writer's accomplishment in the Zen setting.

The amount of time one does Zen practice is not entirely irrelevant to this question, but the quality of one's practice is more important when judging accomplishment. This writer is not particularly well accomplished in Zen even after doing the practice for years. Some years ago I was told that I was roughly at stage three in the ten ox-herding pictures. These pictures are an artistic effort to express differing stages in Zen training without trying to be very serious or philosophical about it. They are useful, however, to indicate to the reader the ability of the writer to "become the phenomenon" of Zen. What this means is that the interpretation of the Zen setting in the present study is located in a context where a middling accomplishment in Zen and the interests of a particular sort of sociologist intersect.

Because the writer is a member of the groups studied and has experienced some change in perspective in the course of time that he has been involved in the practice, the descriptions contained herein need to be located somewhere in the writer's moral career as member. This is so because as one develops under the impact of the practice, one's perceptions of who one is and what is real change as well. This statement is a general comment on the problem encountered when a study of a group uses only accounts of those who have left the organization. The descriptions of the rituals and events in this work are those that are largely shaped by the later years of my involvement in the practice and by my sociological interests, which have also developed over the years. The accounts offered, then, are not just those of the maturing Zen student but also those of the sociologist who attempts to understand his experience in terms of social theory.

The point is that descriptions in this work occur in the context of analysis. They are meant to be honest and adequate descriptions, but clearly they are organized by the analytic context in which they appear. That use is made of a variety of such frames of reference (e.g., symbolic interactionist and constructionist), helps to avoid any entirely one-sided and simplistic organization of experience by theory. This variety of frames of reference matches, I argue, the diversity of experience of Zen practitioners who are at differing stages of Zen practice. The reader needs to look for descriptive detail within the analysis. Chapter V, for example, not only argues for a particular view of Zen practice but contains descriptive information of members' experience and ritual form that are useful for providing a more complete picture of Zen practice that goes well beyond the chapter in which it appears. Many accounts can be generated about the practice; the few that are told in this work are those that seem interesting to the writer as both Zen practitioner and sociologist.

CHAPTER II

A Profile of Zen Membership and Formal Organization in Southern California

Unconventional forms of spirituality have an important place in American history and an enduring appeal to respectable segments of the American population. Ellwood (1979) traces the history of three forms of unconventional and Eastern spirituality in the United States – the Shakers and Spiritualists, Theosophy, and Zen – and allows us to see them and their participants in a favorable light. His analysis has extensively influenced the approach taken in the present study.

Another image of Zen, however, emerges from the association of Zen with various new religious forms that seem foreign and frightening to some. According to some Zen practitioners, this image is held by the less well-informed in our society. It is that of predominantly young persons, dressed in "Asian drag" (as one of my informants put it), isolated from their families, living communally under the influence of a charismatic leader, and engaging in various schemes to raise money for the supposedly nefarious purposes of their organizations, while they neglect their ethnic and religious traditions and sacrifice their rationality. A closer look at the social traits of participants in so-called new religious groups will allow us to see what type of people engage in this activity and how the Zen group is different from others.

A few studies have attempted to characterize the typical member in these groups. Wuthnow (1976, 1976a), for example, reports the results of a study done in the San Francisco Bay Area in 1973 that solicited information on thirteen new religious and quasi-religious groups. He found it useful to present these thirteen groups under three headings. Countercultural groups have in common non-Western or non-Christian origins and include Zen, Transcendental Meditation (TM), Yoga, Iskon (Hare Krishna chanters), and Satanism. Personal growth groups are Western in origin but neutral toward Christianity and include est (Erhard Seminars

Training), Scientology, and Synanon. Neo-Christian groups are new Christian forms and include the Christian World Liberation Front, Children of God, groups that speak in tongues, Jews for Jesus, and the Campus Crusade for Christ. Our focus is mainly on the first set of groups.

Countercultural group members tended to have political attitudes that were radical or liberal, as did members of the personal growth groups; neo-Christians were decidedly more conservative. They had more unconventional lifestyles than did personal growth members who were, in turn, more unconventional than neo-Christian group members. Countercultural group members were more experienced in the use of drugs than both other groupings, with neo-Christians being less experienced and less in favor of legalizing marijuana. They were involved less in conventional religious beliefs and practice than neo-Christians; had more education than neo-Christian group members; and tended to be more geographically mobile, single, and without full-time work than other groups. In all groups, most members were under thirty years of age. Because participants in all these groups, and especially the countercultural groups, were relatively young and had more education than the average American Wuthnow (1976, 292) argued that some participants – Zen members in particular – were creative experimenters in an area of culture that still remains largely undeveloped, not the incompetent and inadvertent victims of manipulative religious movements (Wuthnow, 1976a; also see Tipton, 1982).

The Bay Area is not typical of the country as a whole, however, and only a small proportion of the U.S. population participates in these movements or even knows much about them. But since 1973, when the Bay Area study was done, some evidence has become available showing that this attraction to experience-based religious forms is spreading. For example, a Gallup survey conducted in 1976 found that a large percentage of those polled claimed to be involved in experiential forms of religion in the United States. The findings suggest that at that time approximately ten million people were involved in or practicing faith healing, six million in TM, five million in Yoga, three million in the charismatic movement, three million in "mysticism," and two million in Eastern religion (Gallup, 1979, 116).

These figures lead Carroll to remark that of the six million people involved in TM

Only the United Methodist Church and the Southern Baptist Convention, among Protestants, have larger memberships, and the projected number for Transcendental Meditation is approximately the same as the estimated Jewish population of the United States. These size comparisons are made to indicate the magnitude of the appeal of these movements rather than to imply that such groups necessarily compete with established Churches for members. Many participants in the new movements are also active participants in churches. (Carroll & Roozen, 1979, 25)

Despite this evidence, however, it is difficult to take such claims very seriously. Saying that one is involved and practicing is easy, but there may be little involvement beyond the words. The next table in the Gallup report helps make the point. The survey asked, "Would you say that you have been 'born again' or have had a 'born again' experience – that is, a turning point in your life when you committed yourself to Christ?" Thirty-four percent of those asked said "yes," which seems a rather large number. But when broken down by age – 42 percent of primary school children, for example, said "yes" – what is being measured becomes much less clear. What needs to be recognized is that a distinction must be made between kinds of religious activity. We do not address the experiences of primary school children (and others in this context) when we examine groups such as Zen practitioners. Although both may indeed be "experiential" in some sense, the differences are certainly greater than the similarities. Let us turn elsewhere for some finer-grained details on this sort of religious activity and its practitioners in the United States.

Another study, also done in the Bay Area (Tipton, 1982), examines three settings, one in each of Wuthnow's types – neo-Christian, countercultural (Tipton calls these neo-Oriental), and personal growth. This report tends to confirm Wuthnow's results. The group members are typically younger, very much influenced by the counterculture (Tipton did his research in the mid- to late-1970s), politically liberal, and well educated. Neo-Christians were predominantly lower-middle and working-class "hip dropouts," est was largely middle-middle class, and Zen was upper-middle class "bohemian hip-seekers." Tipton's main concern is how the various groups provide each member with a way, a set of beliefs and practices, that allows the member to make moral sense of the world.

A student of Bellah, Tipton sees the rise of new religious movements as being directly related to the increasing moral ambiguity and decline of centralized ideology and civil religion in the United States. He finds that not only do the three groups differ in terms of background of their members, but each group has a different moral style – a decidedly different way of making sense of the world.

The neo-Christian group, which had the more conservative background and more members with only high-school educations, had a moral view that was based on standard Christian notions of good and evil, divine authority as the source of principled ethics (commandments), and a view of human nature that is evil but perfectible. This group's neo-Christian quality can be most clearly seen in its evangelical practices and beliefs. The est group, less alienated from American society than either of the other two, drew from a wide range of persons and had a moral view that was highly eclectic. It combined recent therapeutic notions and practices with a variety of religious theories, in addition to situational rules and a calculation of what produces the best consequences for self. Tipton describes est's belief system as "psychologized monist individualism."

The Zen group had a monistic belief system – that is, one that explicitly avoids such dualisms as good and evil, and person and God. Emphasis was not upon belief, however, but on intuition, oriented to the present and based on a rigorous and demanding meditational practice. He sees this group doing what feels right rather than following "commandments" or calculating consequences (Tipton, 1982, 14–20). This compatibility explains the attraction that neo-Oriental groups have had for disillusioned countercultural "seekers."

A Profile of Zen Membership

The two Zen groups studied herein are located in Southern California and have been the subject of two previous sociological reports (Preston 1981, 1982).[1] The writer is a member of both groups and has been for some years. The materials on members found in this section are the product of two series of interviews; the first done in the summer of 1980, the second begun in the summer of 1984. The emphasis in this section is on describing the Zen students themselves.[2]

I interviewed members of two Zen groups, one in Los Angeles and one in San Diego, in an attempt to represent the groups as a whole but also on the basis of convenience. My goal is to describe the social characteristics of Zen practitioners as clearly as possible and to give the reader the materials with which to build an image of typical Zen students in southern California, and perhaps in the United States as a whole. Before beginning this description, a few terms used in the text and in the Appendix summary need to be clarified.

The two groups studied are referred to as the Los Angeles Center and the San Diego Center. The Los Angeles group with a Japanese Zen teacher has been the core group with which various other Zen groups, such as the one in San Diego, have affiliated informally. These groups can be found in Santa Barbara, Tucson, Los Gatos, Mexico City, and elsewhere. During the last decade the San Diego group has had an informal yet close relationship with the Los Angeles organization, and then a legal relationship as a branch of the Los Angeles group. Now, as a result of recent difficulties, the San Diego group operates as an autonomous, democratically run entity.

The size of these two groups has grown considerably during the last ten years. The Appendix shows the "practicing membership" (235) at the Los Angeles group in 1980. Practicing members are defined by a membership fee schedule (twenty-five dollars per month in 1980) and by the privilege of seeing a teacher (the roshi in the years before the number of members became prohibitively large) regularly in a private interview *(dokusan)*. "Practicing members" also include the residents of the Center (89 in 1980) but not corresponding members. San Diego group "members" (those who paid monthly dues of thirty dollars in 1984) number 69.

In the period following 1983 both groups went through a transition with the Los Angeles group losing members (especially long-term senior residents) and the San Diego group gaining members (initially at least). Part of the growth of the San Diego group can be understood as the result of this group recently gaining a teacher in residence. She finished her training in Los Angeles in 1983 where she had been seeing students in interviews for some years. Many of these same students were, and continue to be, members of the San Diego group. At least ten of the sixty-nine San Diego members were recent residents of the Los Angeles Center who moved to be with their teacher and for other reasons.

The following interview summaries, based on the Appendix data, are divided into three groups: a 1980 sample of forty-seven members from both the Los Angeles and San Diego groups; a 1980 sample of fourteen new members of the San Diego group; and a 1984 sample of fourteen new members of the San Diego group.

According to the Los Angeles data, Zen appeals to persons chiefly between the ages of twenty-five and forty (see Appendix). Residents at the Los Angeles Center in 1980, as well as practicing members as a whole, were concentrated in this age span. Although many were older than forty, almost none were younger than twenty-five and none were younger than twenty-one. The two samples of "newer" members in San Diego in both 1980 and 1984 do not indicate any changes in ages at which new members joined. In the two samples, there were four and three new members between twenty and thirty years of age in 1980 and 1984 respectively; seven and seven between thirty and forty years of age, and three and four between forty and fifty years of age.

Both groups have more men than women, but the difference is slight. In 1980 practicing members of the Los Angeles group (residents excepted) numbered seventy-eight men and sixty-eight women. The same pattern held among residents although exact numbers are not available for this group. The San Diego group had forty-one men and twenty-eight women in 1984. Until recently it was commonly thought by practitioners that the Zen setting was one where the sexual discrimination typical of the broader U.S. society was largely avoided. The realization that sex has indeed been grounds for special treatment, even by Zen teachers, has resulted in disillusionment and bitterness among some practitioners.[3]

Zen practice is done largely by persons who are single or divorced; for those who are married, only one spouse usually participates. According to the results of all sixty-one interviews, there were nineteen married couples of whom only three had both spouses involved in Zen practice; one of these three couples had met and married while residents at a Zen Center. This latter pattern is more common now that Zen residence groups have been in existence for a decade or so. Among San Diego members, for example, of ten practicing couples six of them met and became couples in a Zen context. A few married members interviewed, however, expressed the opinion that Zen practice was making their relationship with their spouses more difficult. More commonly, however, practitioners see Zen practice as a way of stabilizing their lives and solidifying commitments.

Contrary to the Bay Area study's findings, most Zen practitioners in our groups work full-time. In the 1980 sample, fourteen of the thirty-six combined full- and part-time workers were employed as staff at the Los Angeles Center. The eleven listed as unemployed (in the Appendix) were a mixed group with only four unemployed in the usual sense of the term (i.e., looking for work); the other seven included two housewives, a student, a retired person, and three who were unemployed temporarily by choice. In the 1984 sample, none could afford the luxury of not working.

The typical Zen student is highly educated. In the 1980 sample twenty-five out of forty-seven have some graduate schooling and only three have less than a high school education. This same sample showed eighteen persons with college degrees, nine with Masters degrees, and eight with doctoral degrees. Teachers and scientists are common. In addition, nearly all practitioners are white, middle-class, urban, and liberal. This striking degree of homogeneity of background and experience enables a rare level of communication in talks by teachers and in informal interaction among students. That these same persons are often aware of the limits of discursive speech allows them a positive approach to meditative practices.

The counterculture of the 1960s is still recognized as influencing new Zen members. Some are now too young to have had much exposure to it but still eight of fourteen in the 1984 sample saw the counterculture as a strong influence in their lives. One still wears long hair and a beard; another lived in the Haight-Ashbury district in the 1960s; others mention a connection with the antiwar movement. Almost all Zen practitioners have used marijuana and half of them have experimented with psychedelic drugs. What is interesting, however, is that almost no one in the 1984 sample saw a connection between psychedelic experience and their attraction to Zen. Although the "spiritual" meaning of psychedelic drugs has diminished since the 1960s, it is difficult for this writer to imagine the counterculture without the spiritual dimension of psychedelics.

Although nearly all practitioners admit to a radical or liberal background, characterizing their current political philosophy is more complex. In the 1980 sample, twenty-six of forty-seven say they could not label themselves simply as radical, liberal, moderate, or conservative. (The question of political identification was not asked in the 1984 series of interviews.) This group of twenty-six had various difficulties placing themselves on such a scale. Some said they were liberal on some issues, conservative on others. Others offered a critique of such a question and the assumptions that lay behind it. Some were disarming in such observations as:

I don't know what the difference between conservative and radical means or if they are relevant. (no. 11)

This particular comment, coming from a well-educated and accomplished practitioner, remains difficult to dismiss. It reminds us of the limits of what passes for thought and knowledge in everyday life.

The near unanimity of a radical–liberal political sensibility among practitioners and its transformation in the direction of greater subtlety is a point that supports the theory of Wilber (1981, 1983). He predicts a movement away from parochial sentiments and moral judgments to universalistic sentiments, and finally to an experience of and identity with "spirit" as meditation is practiced.

To what degree have Zen practitioners shopped around in the "spiritual marketplace"? Are they involved in other therapeutic or new religious groups? About one-quarter of those interviewed had no involvement with any such activity other than Zen. The same proportion was involved in three or more other forms, and about one-half of all members had done est training, which was offered free to the Los Angeles Center staff members at one time. Although these figures might be interpreted in a way that makes Zen look rather "new age" in style – what others have called the human potential movement (Stone, 1976) and Wuthnow calls personal growth movements – they also permit an opposing interpretation.

A hallmark of the movement is the extent of multiple participation and eclectic borrowing among these organizations and disciplines.... While the disciplines are distinct, they are usually complementary, and many people enroll in several groups in the same period. For instance, one leader of encounter groups who has been Rolfed and who participated in the Arica Training is receiving Gestalt therapy in exchange for Swedish massage and Polarity therapy. (Stone, 1976, 94, 99)

Participants in the new age movement also tend to be more concerned with physical fitness and nutrition and are willing to spend considerable amounts of money to accumulate the commodities and lifestyles that are associated with this new ideal. This is largely an upper-middle-class movement as is Zen but one much less apologetic in its display of affluence.

This attitude contrasts strikingly with that of most Zen practitioners. Although Zen practitioners often share interests with the new age movement, the degree of commitment to a daily practice in Zen is such that other interests and activities tend to take on secondary importance. Even though there are few rules about lifestyles at Zen centers, the demands of the practice tend to impose a common form. For those living at a Zen center (and about one-half of those interviewed in this study are or were doing so), the daily schedule of meditation and work is sufficiently rigorous to absorb one's energies. Also the countercultural style that still prevails at the center studied is antithetical to typical patterns of upper-middle-class consumption. Even more basic, in embracing first counter-cultural ideals and second Zen practice, many have given up professional careers for blue-collar jobs and simply cannot afford an affluent lifestyle. (See the Appendix for details on participation in other therapeutic and new religious groups.)

Some difference in involvement in other groups was indicated in the 1984 sample (although it is not evident in the Appendix summary). Ten of fourteen members claimed having little or no involvement in other activities, but this disguises an interesting point. Although the sample is small, more persons entered Zen practice with therapeutic motives in 1984 than in 1980. Fewer "spiritual" motives were given for beginning Zen practice. However, this emphasis on Zen's therapeutic benefits matches to a degree the psychological style of Zen teaching in San Diego and may reflect nothing more.

This description of Zen practitioners is based on the first part of the interview schedule and provides materials for thinking about Zen students in terms of what has been called a "passivist" perspective (Heirich, 1977). It provides answers to questions like: "Is participation in Zen determined, caused by, or correlated with, sex, age, class, education, or exposure to psychedelic experience?" Such questions are expected when first approaching the phenomenon. After becoming more acquainted with the setting, the questions often change from "Why do they do this?" to "How do they do it?" This switch in perspective informed the construction of the second part of the interview schedule, which deals with conversion/ commitment themes, the results of which will be discussed in later chapters. Now, however, I will offer a sketch of the physical layout of one of the centers discussed.

The Physical Layout of a Zen Center

The Los Angeles Center[4] is located in a rundown residential area in west-central Los Angeles. Tall palm trees line the street and old hotels, now tenements, remind one of earlier, more prosperous times. Its proximity to arterial streets and to downtown Los Angeles makes the sounds of sirens and police helicopters common. In general the noise level of a central city prevails. In the summer the smog is heavy and the temperature rises regularly into the nineties. The Santa Anna winds of September and October provide a temporary respite from the smog but not the heat. The neighborhood lies just on the edge of a commercial area most recently used by Koreans and it partakes to some extent of the stability and prosperity of this commercial area. It remains, however, a multiethnic and multiracial area with large numbers of single men who use the streets, especially at night, for their own activities. It is what most people consider to be unsafe (certainly Zen Center members do), and there have been rapes and a murder on the block on which the Center is located.

The Center itself is made up of a collection of homes and apartment houses that are all on the same block. Originally one home was acquired by the teacher and a few students in 1967. Since then, as membership has grown, two other homes were acquired to accommodate the demands for living space. Finally, three apartment houses were acquired and two of these remodeled. The conversion of one extremely run-down tenement had a settling influence on the block. Center buildings have fairly recent paint jobs and roofs; those in good condition required no changes. Some have had their landscaping altered to approximate a Japanese style. Pine trees are trimmed in the oriental style, and there is a fish pond in front of one of the main buildings. Two signs announce the Center and the affiliated institute.

In 1982 about 125 members lived on this block and some 25 others lived within a few blocks in apartments and homes. Because several of these homes and apartment buildings are contiguous and abut one another, practically the entire block is dominated by the Center. People who live nearby usually appreciate the Center despite its early rising schedule and other anomalies. Center members are well mannered and the grounds well kept. One red-brick tenement overlooks a central area of the Center property. What the occupants of this building think of the Center's activities is no doubt mixed, but the sounds on hot summer nights, especially on weekends, provide a definite contrast with the mildly Japanese and Anglo flavor of the Center. In the middle of an outdoor celebration at the Center, a visiting Japanese official was giving a speech, when the comment came down from the fifth floor, "Ah baloooooney, mann!" That comment, which probably sums up the sentiments of a part

The sangha house containing the Center's kitchen and other common facilities with the Japanese-style fish pond in front.

of the neighborhood, was taken on this occasion by Center members good-humoredly as harmless disdain.

Moving onto the property and inside the buildings at the Center, one senses a contrast from the usual public image of Japanese Zen. Although there is some effort to cultivate the grounds in Japanese ways, for the most part the landscaping is practical. Lawns are maintained and trees have been planted, but only the inside of the roshi's residence, tastefully done in an upper-middle-class way, might be called fancy. Almost every place else reflects a mildly impoverished limitation on decoration and style. One can also detect an unwillingness to fuss or decorate beyond the personally interesting and the minimal standards of comfort. The surroundings resemble student accommodations without self-indulgence. Arrangements are comfortable but just a little run down. There are good reasons for this other than personal tastes. The Center has been committed to allowing more people to live at the Center so they can practice daily with the teacher. To meet the demand, the Center has expanded at a rate that finds it almost constantly overextended financially. There is not much fat, not much affluence. Members' automobiles tend to be five to ten years old, and somewhat neglected cosmetically. Center facilities in general have been undergoing constant modification in an effort to meet new demands for space. Walls have been removed, floors refinished, windows enlarged, foundations strengthened, roofs replaced, kitchens added, garbage areas improved, and refrigeration facilities expanded. Zen in America, at least in this group, is not affluent.

A medical clinic was established some years ago to meet the general medical needs of members and is offered free to the many needy persons in the neighborhood. It takes advantage of one or two physicians who have moved to the Center to do Zen practice and others with medically relevant skills and experience.

In personal expression, especially ceramics and woodworking, Zen practitioners find a Japanese aesthetic appealing. This aesthetic is visible at the Center in both public and private areas. It symbolizes the present state of syncretism between Japanese and American culture in Zen settings. One would expect this dominance of the Japanese element to become much less influential as non-Japanese Zen teachers establish their own Centers and produce their own students. Even where it is not visible in physical objects, however, Japanese cultural influence manifests itself in very subtle ways. D. T. Suzuki notes that Japanese culture is very thoroughly Zen culture. Seen in this light, separating Zen from Japanese cultural forms might be difficult. It is clear, however, that the forms Zen takes in America will certainly become less Japanese. What Zen is, different from the Japanese forms that it is now associated with, is an empirical question that is only answered in retrospect.

The core of the Center, the meditation hall or *zendo,* is located in the ground floor of a large, two-story house that has had nearly all of its interior walls removed to provide an open sitting space. The present layout is the result of several remodelings that were done to accommodate more people and makes maximum use of the space. The white interior of the zendo and the many windows give the room a relatively open and light feeling. The refinished oak floors creak and snap when walked on, reflecting years of hard use. There is a central altar area where incense is burned and flowers stand in front of an image that is curiously ambiguous in origin and meaning. No doubt it is a representation of human qualities in a particular form of the Buddha. The altar is a special space, treated like altars in other settings. There are ways of moving and holding the body in the proximity of the altar that are prescribed. "Don't walk in front of it, or if you do then do a slight bow in its direction" is a typical admonition.

With the exception of the altar, the zendo space is reserved entirely for its main function, sitting in meditation *(zazen)*. The perimeter of the room is covered with black mats *(zabutans)* about three feet square. An individual is assigned one of these mats and, for most meditation periods, sits facing the wall on a small, round black cushion *(zafu)*. Because there is space for additional *zabutans,* the zendo can accommodate a surprisingly large number of people. A talk by the roshi, for example, sometimes finds all floor space covered by mats. A second house converted to handle the overflow of sitters has come to be crowded as well.

The teacher sits in a central location in front of the altar when not in a separate room giving private interviews. The term used to refer to such interviews and the prescribed way of entering and exiting them varies with the rank of the particular teacher. *Dokusan* (going alone) is the general Japanese term for this kind of interaction with a roshi. In the group studied, there are so many students that the roshi gives *dokusan* in one room and one of his senior students gives interviews in a room upstairs. Despite the crowded conditions and the importance of quiet for sitting, the comings and goings of students to both teachers can be handled surprisingly well. This smooth flow of people in such close proximity to one another is clearly related to Japanese skills and sensitivities. Their ability to live in very crowded conditions in very civilized ways is well known. It is no small accomplishment for Americans to learn these skills and sensitivities because, as any American who has visited Japan knows, we are indeed "barbarians" in our relatively unorganized habits of individualistic expression and use of space. Whether this ability has anything to do with "Zen," of course, is another question entirely, although it seems obvious that the Japanese forms of Zen's social organization in this country are not irrelevant to what members call "the practice," and Bourdieu (1977) calls "habitus."

Immediately adjacent to the zendo, across a driveway, another house of similar style and vintage contains the kitchen and commons area. This was the first house purchased and it too has seen many remodelings over the years. Shortly after its purchase, a fish pond of Japanese inspiration was dug in the small front yard, and it remains today, populated by koi (Japanese carp), lotus blossums, and algae that all but takes over in the warm weather. A sign in Spanish requests the neighborhood children not to bother the fish, but this request is very loosely honored by the children who often play there. A sitting porch, with an old couch and a couple of overstuffed chairs badly in need of repair, overlook the pond and members are often found sitting there reading a newspaper, eating lunch, or drinking coffee. It is the most public front of the Center and visitors usually come there looking for information or residents. I have heard members describe this commons house, as well as the zendo, as "funky." It is a little run down and very casual and populated by people dressed in black sitting skirts or robes (both men and women). Neighbors are used to it, but it takes the eye of passers-by at times. Inside, what was the living room is now a coffee area that becomes a food line at meal times. The kitchen and dishwashing machine take up the rest of this floor, along with refrigeration units and food preparation areas. The second story is a commons area where members can watch television, sit on the carpeted floor, eat meals, or whatever. In good weather, the backyard, which is planted in grass and contained by recently (1979) planted redwood trees, is also used for eating meals. The kitchen prepares three meals a day, which residents share according to arrangements made with the Center. Visitors are asked to pay a fee (a small box is placed conspicuously where the food is served), which was three dollars a meal in 1980. Food is self-served from large containers placed on a table in the commons house and each person cleans up after oneself in the dishwasher room and leaves the utensils to be steam cleaned.

The administrative tasks of the Center are done in offices in an old red-brick apartment house that has been remodeled. Most rooms and small apartments in this building are used as living space for residents of the Center, but some more centrally located rooms are used as offices. The bookstore, reception area, buildings maintenance shop, sewing room, the institute, and the medical clinic are all located here. As in all Center buildings and nearby apartments, considerable care is taken to keep doors and windows locked during off hours because theft is a common occurrence in the neighborhood. Room keys given to visitors to the Center often have police whistles attached to their rings, further indicating the realities of the area.

Formal Organization and Staff

The Center is organized as a tax-exempt religious corporation. The roshi, born and trained in Japan, is both the president and the spiritual leader. Before the mid-1984 changes, he selected twenty-one voting members from among the members of the Center who in turn elected the Board of Directors. This board makes policy for the Center and elects the officers of the corporation who handle the secular activities of the Center.

An affiliated institute is qualified to grant undergraduate degrees and presently functions as an organization for encouraging and sponsoring Buddhist studies. A publishing house (Center Publications) was established in the early 1970s but was phased out to improve the financial situation of the organization in the mid- to late 1970s.

The number of residents on staff at the Center grew to be quite large. Even after cutbacks the staff numbered 40 of the roughly 125 residents in mid-1983. These staff members usually were paid a token amount but their room and board was covered as were fees normally charged for participation in Center practices such as *sesshins* (retreats). The bulk of the staff included people doing advertising, layout, and editorial work for the publishing house; those doing the woodworking, plumbing, electrical work, and painting essential for making old buildings livable; and the office workers essential to running an organization with more than 200 members. The medical clinic was another small but important function. Besides staff reduction during the period of financial cutbacks, other members were asked to "work out," that is to take full-time jobs as carpenters, plumbers, electricians, painters, and landscapers and to donate their wages to the Center. Many did this and these services are offered today under such rubrics as "Zen Carpentry." Those who did this work followed a demanding schedule. Like other Center practitioners, they awoke at 4:30 or 5:00 A.M., sat in *zazen* for about two hours, ate breakfast, went to work for eight or more hours, returned to the Center in time to eat, and then sat for two more hours.

Spiritual or "religious" activities at the Center are managed directly by roshi according to a monastic organization of Zen practices in Japan, which consists of a core of roles that ensure that the rituals are done smoothly. Anyone who wants can learn these "positions" as they are called and, in fact, all are encouraged to do so. In the event that no previous arrangements have been made, a senior person usually assigns these various positions by circulating among those who plan to sit. It is considered good practice to do these positions, which include timekeeper *(jikido)*, bell ringer *(densho)*, chant leader *(ino)*, and others, depending upon the formality of the occasion.

Roshi has connections with several different Zen traditions in Japan, but his main organizational connection is with the Soto branch and Eiheiji temple. For practical purposes this is not very relevant, but one notices these connections when a senior student is formally received as a successor to the teacher. Some of the ceremonies take place in Japan. As one might suspect, missionary activity in a foreign country rarely loses complete contact with the home organization, and the money provided from time to time for the development of Zen in this country tends to maintain the contact.

CHAPTER III

The Zen Teacher

The view of a Zen teacher, a roshi, presented in this chapter, is considerably more mundane than that usually available in Zen literature. By examining one particular Zen teacher in various situations in the course of a typical day, I have attempted to show how members come to experience the teacher as a secular and spiritual authority.

Not all Zen teachers, students, or groups are the same. The role of the teacher in Zen depends, among other things, on the kinds of students available. It is generally recognized by those familiar with the situation that relatively few persons in Japan today are genuinely interested in doing Zen practice. Although the number of members of Zen sects remains high (Basabe, Shin, & Lanzaco, 1968, 5–6), few members actually do *zazen* and other practices. This distinction is crucial for understanding and describing what is happening with Zen in the United States today.

The roshi in this study regularly notes in his talks and writings that the actual practice of *zazen* is considerably stronger in the United States and other Western countries than it is in Japan. The word "decadent" is sometimes used to describe the condition of Zen in Japan. Although there is no shortage of Zen priests, their activities are often limited to ceremonial functions on weekends and religious holidays or to funeral rites. Buddhism in Japan is considered to be the religion that deals especially with the rites of the grave and thus almost all Japanese consider themselves Buddhist in this regard. It is difficult for any form of religious life to remain viable in such a situation of ceremonial objectification and specialization, and especially difficult for Zen.

In the United States, in contrast to Japan, the kind of Zen practice that has been most appealing to its members is of a very different sort. Instead of a weekend or ceremony-oriented activity, Zen in the United States is based on a daily practice that extends directly into the activities of everyday life. As such it tends to meet the same kinds of needs that those who are attracted to so-called new religious forms have, which are often not met by the established churches. These needs are for a less institutionalized, less objectified spiritual form than is often found in the mainline churches. Those churches that have experienced the most vitality (reflected in membership growth) in recent years, for example, are just those who offer the possibility of an experience of spirituality. Other forms of new religious activity that are less conservative but also experiential meet the needs of those with less fundamentalist dispositions or who feel out of place in the standard church setting.

The kind of Zen practice that has been developing in the United States is a community practice. Individuals and families often move together to form a community, when possible around a teacher, in order to support one another's practice. This particular form of community practice can be found in many Zen groups in this country. Such groups can be found in Los Angeles, San Francisco, Rochester, Santa Rosa, Providence, and elsewhere. The daily schedule typically includes about four hours of *zazen* along with a full day of work practice *(samu)* with regular interviews with a teacher (where one is in residence) and monthly retreats. This practice is rigorous and requires a commitment far beyond that which most persons are willing to make. It resembles the sort of religious life that is found more often in monasteries than among the laity. This form is largely the creation of the Japanese teachers who have come to this country in the last twenty-five years and their American students.

Zen teachers, who are endorsed by their training organizations without qualification, are called "roshi" (teacher). The person who holds this title is someone who has not simply fulfilled the requirements for a credential but also one who has been endorsed by their teacher as sharing a particular quality of Mind. What is being transmitted, it is said, is not just the written word, not the sutras, not the objectified propositional knowledge, beliefs, and practices, but an embodied quality of Mind and of Being. One speaks of the quality of Mind as being the same from the historical Buddha ("Buddha" means enlightened one; "historical" refers to Shakyamuni Buddha) to the present teacher, the lineage being traced back through particular sects and particular teachers. The student who is endorsed as a successor to a teacher is recognized as embodying the quality of the teachings as that lineage and teacher manifests it. The process of this recognition is institutionalized in various stages from being a "dharma holder," to "dharma successor," to being "sensei," to being fully recognized as "roshi."

In the abstract this resembles the principle of legitimation used for popes who are seen as successors to the special relationship the Apostle

Peter had with Christ. Zen teachers thus carry a charisma of office that is potentially much more powerful than that of a parish priest. Each bearer of the title "roshi" supposedly has actualized a quality of Mind similar if not identical to that of the historical Buddha. This brings the myth – in Joseph Campbell's (1968, 3) sense of the word as "the secret opening through which the inexhaustible energies of the cosmos pour into human cultural manifestation" – closer to home, to everyday life, and provides a powerful support for a daily practice and the demands it makes. Further, the claim that anyone and everyone can realize this quality of Mind makes it especially appealing to American students. For American Zen students, who have been raised in a culture where universalistic standards are an ideal, this openness to all – this recognition that sex, age, social class, and race have little bearing on accomplishing the way – is a powerful element in their accepting of the authority of the teacher in Zen.

Zen Buddhism in Japan is organized into two main sects called Rinzai and Soto. These sects have separate organizations and different traditions that reflect preferred ways of practicing and teaching based on two important Zen teachers and their descendants. Members of the Rinzai sect look back to the Chinese master Lin-Chi (d. 866) as the founder and have come to emphasize the vigorous examination of koans as their main form of practice. The Soto sect takes the Japanese master Dogen (d. 1253) as its founder and, along with some other features, is usually seen as preferring *shikan taza* or "just sitting" to koan study. For all practical purpose, however, these distinctions can be ignored in our study, because Zen practice in the United States is usually a mixture of these various techniques. The teacher in the group studied herein regularly emphasizes the irrelevance of sectarian differences in Zen practice and, because of his own training in both traditions, usually seeks a balance of practices from both schools.

At the same time, however, the roshi in this study has maintained a connection with Soto Zen in Japan in that the Los Angeles Center is a recognized Soto Zen temple and training center and he is a fully recognized abbot. He has continued to observe the rules and regulations of Soto headquarters in conducting the religious affairs of the Center. He explains this in the following terms (paraphrased from a talk by the roshi).[1] Zen in America will certainly take on its own unique forms as it does in any new culture. What is to be changed and what retained are not yet clear. The connection with Japan and the Soto organization feels right. As new Zen centers are developed under his guidance, however, this connection to Japan is something that depends on the members themselves. One such Center in New York has no connection to Japan whereas another in San Diego originally did. Nothing in either situation cannot be changed as the members choose.

The Teacher

Taizan Maezumi-roshi was born in 1931 in a Zen temple where his father was head priest. He was raised in this setting and ordained at the age of eleven as a monk in the Soto sect of Zen Buddhism. During high school, he began studying with a Zen lay teacher who never became a Zen priest, something quite unusual. This lay roshi, Koryu-roshi, was instructed by his teacher to work with lay persons in an effort to rejuvenate Zen practice in Japan. Maezumi-roshi moved into this Center and practiced with Koryu-

Maezumi-roshi, abbot of the Los Angeles Center, during a work period.

roshi while he was attending college at Komazawa University in Tokyo. This experience was to have a lasting influence.

Maezumi-roshi graduated from college with degrees in Asian literature and philosophy and went on to continue his Zen training at Sojiji, one of the two main Soto Zen monasteries in Japan. In 1955 he received dharma transmission from his father, Hakujun Kuroda-roshi.

In 1956 he came to the U.S. and served for some time as a priest at the Soto Zen Temple in Los Angeles, a largely Japanese-American congregation where priests have mainly ritual duties. The kinds of members and activities at this temple are strikingly different from the Center he later founded. While *zazen* is the main interest and activity at the Center, the temple activity could be classified as more typically churchlike. This transition for Maezumi-roshi was a movement into an area of practice that was not at all well established in Japan and certainly not in the United States at that time. It came to be what we have called a community-based practice, which integrates both monastic and lay elements. Roshi spent some time working in a factory, learning the language (which is still less than perfect), got married, and, some years later, divorced. In 1966 he founded the Center. Soon after this he finished study with two different Zen teachers in the Rinzai tradition, Koryu Osaka-roshi and Hakuun Yasutani-roshi, and received their approval to teach on his own. He eventually remarried and presently has three children. The family lives on the block where the other Center buildings are located.

Maezumi-roshi is a Japanese man of athletic build, relatively short, with a shaved head in the style of Zen monks. When he is not doing physical work on the grounds, he often wears a garment that resembles the cassock Catholic priests wear. When traveling with his family, he dresses more casually – checkered shirts, cotton pants, black shoes. There is nothing particularly unusual about him and he appears ordinary in many ways. He is in his mid-fifties but often seems younger. He smiles readily and has a good sense of humor. His home is tastefully decorated in a combination of Japanese and American styles. For years he and his family drove his wife's Volkswagen bus, but when this wore out, the group organized a fundraiser to buy them a small Oldsmobile. He does not drive himself, or at least I have never seen him do so. His life is almost entirely oriented to the Center with the exception of entertaining visitors from Japan, traveling with the family to the mountains for a weekend, or on trips to other Zen groups in the United States, Europe, and Mexico.

Daily Schedule

The daily schedule of the teacher in the group in Los Angeles begins at 5:00 A.M. He rises, dresses, and has tea with the assistance of an attendant, and proceeds to the zendo where students are already in their places waiting to begin an hour and a half of *zazen*. The teacher enters the zendo, inspects by walking in front of those sitting and returns to his seat. The period begins and the teacher, usually after waiting some minutes, leaves the zendo to go to the interview room. *Dokusan* (the private interview with the teacher) involves students going one at a time to see the teacher to ask questions regarding their practice and to have their understanding tested. During this time the teacher sits in the physically demanding full lotus position. At the end of this time, a short service with chanting and offering of incense is led either by the roshi or one of his senior students. Breakfast is then served in the zendo, but the teacher usually leaves to have breakfast with his family.

After a work period of an hour and a half or so, the roshi returns to the zendo at 10:30 A.M. for more sitting with students who are participating in a special training period *(ango)*. At noon this sitting ends, lunch is served and the afternoon is free from ritual activities. During this time the roshi is usually involved in administrative matters, handles correspondence with various persons in several countries on both practical and spiritual matters, and spends time with his family. At 7:00 P.M. the sitting schedule is resumed in the zendo until 9 P.M.

During each month there is a period of ten days organized as a special intensive practice period called *sesshin* (roughly, retreat). A common form of organization is to have a seven-day *sesshin* and another three-day *sesshin* every month. The teacher's schedule during this time begins at 4 A.M. He rises and pursues the same schedule as described above but this time, after lunch and a break, he returns to the zendo for more *dokusan* from 2:30 until 5:00 P.M. He returns to the zendo again at 7:00 P.M. for still more *dokusan* and the day ends at 9:00 P.M. Nearly the entire day is spent sitting in the lotus position in a small room, seeing students one after another. Maintenance of such a demanding schedule during one-third of each month makes clear the teacher's commitment to his students and emphasizes the distinction mentioned previously between involvement in a church on the one hand and a daily practice on the other. Again it is the availability of students who are willing to do the more demanding practices that allows the teacher to be something more than an official in a formal organization.

Interaction with Students

For purposes of description and analysis we will deal with three kinds of teacher–student encounters. We use this information to communicate a notion of what occurs in the Zen setting, but also to begin to understand how authority is produced and maintained. *Informal interaction* between student and teacher can be found during common work projects, meetings, parties, shared informal meals, and so on. Because of its social context, this form of interaction is particularly fateful for the student. It is commonly assumed that the usual interaction rituals of everyday life will be observed, and to the extent that they are not, one can experience self-mortification. The breaches of interaction ritual are initiated by the teacher and at times are memorable enough to become part of the group's folklore. *Diplomatic interaction* is a form of polite encounter, limited to safe topics and predictable forms. *Formal interviews (dokusan)* are highly structured yet highly spontaneous. One is encouraged to express one's understanding in direct, nonreflective ways, but the exchange can be as mundane as asking directions from a stranger. These interviews are private and what occurs in them is considered confidential. Let us look at some examples of these sorts of student–teacher interactions.

Informal Interaction

In informal interaction with the roshi some years ago, one of my informants had the following experience.

Some weeks earlier I had given him a birthday gift of a case of wine that I had selected for him. Wine was a hobby of mine at the time and I took some pains to select a variety of relatively cheap but interesting California wines. I was interested in his reaction to it since I thought it particularly nice. After receiving it he brought it up in conversation and thanked me for my "thoughtful" gift. I began immediately to talk of the various wines and their particular individual characteristics. Without a word he walked away from me and I was left midsentence, talking to no one. At the time I was a bit stunned, but soon interpreted the meaning of his behavior as a case of a Zen teacher's unpredictability or unconventionality and of my own position of lack of accomplishment in Zen. I wondered if I had done something to cause this response or if he did that with others as a matter of course. I never really answered this question but I came, in time, to understand it as a direct, nonverbal comment upon my "picking and choosing" regarding the wine. (no. 26)

   This incident is particularly interesting because such a direct violation of interaction ritual (walking away from a one-on-one conversation in midsentence) is rare in everyday life. As Goffman (1967) has pointed out, such ritual is directly functional for preserving the sacredness of the performing self, and is only rarely, and then only under specific conditions, violated. More common is the observance of ritual proprieties, while withholding support of the performance in other less direct ways. The roshi's willingness to violate such conventions is entirely consistent with his role as teacher to students studying the self (as Zen practice is often described) and has an impact that is not soon forgotten. That such behavior is acceptable is an indication of his authority among his students, who then interpret his action as an example of him teaching them directly about the nature of the self. To those less committed to doing Zen practice and working with the roshi, this breaching of conventional, self-preserving behavior might seem illegitimate.

Another example of informal interaction with different impact occurred when roshi visited me and my wife at our home. Some time during the stay he asked to see where I sit (do *zazen*). I took him to my office/ sitting room and showed him the corner where I sit. A framed rubbing of a brass bodhisatva hung on the wall and the usual square black mat and round sitting cushion were on the floor below it. When I showed him this place I was a bit uncertain as to what he might say about it. In fact, he said nothing but did a standing bow from the waist with his hands in what the Japanese call *gassho* (which resembles the Christian posture of prayer). I was struck by his gesture, which would have been perfectly appropriate and expected in a more pretentious setting, one more decorated or ambitiously devotional. In this corner of my house, however, despite the fact that I had spent thousands of hours sitting on this very spot in *zazen,* his bow was totally unexpected. Its effect was to communicate immediately that this was not a typical "social" encounter where one is showing another the house but an opportunity to emphasize that important activities relevant to the values we share are done on this spot and that the realities symbolized in the rubbing that hangs on the wall are alive in our relationship. I was nonplussed, a bit stunned by again being instructed in the subtlest way by his behavior. Again I asked myself, "How am I to interact with this man?"

That I took the bow as an important lesson instead of a commonplace gesture by a Buddhist priest is understandable in terms of my membership as a Zen practitioner, my relationship with this teacher, and my own practice of sitting in that particular location. The descriptions of the social organization of Zen practice and its consequences undertaken in this study are an effort to come to understand this and similar encounters more clearly.

Diplomatic Interaction

Examples of diplomatic interactions are common but not particularly illuminating. Diplomatic interactions such as rituals of greeting take standard, recognizable forms such as:

Hello, David.
Hello, roshi.
Everything all right with you?
Sure, just fine.

Your family?
Oh yeah. Just great.
Good. Give my best to Jeana.
I will.
O.K. See you.

Formal Interview Interaction

Lining up to see the teacher in *dokusan* and waiting as next in line to go in, a student is often in a state of uncertainty or ambivalence as to how to be with the teacher. Using the standard coping mechanisms of everyday life, a student might attempt to be clever, modest, obsequious, relaxed. This attempt can generate considerable energy, especially when one is also working on a riddle or a task that has no possible intellectual solution. Because the fatefulness of the situation may seem immense, students sometimes avoid these interviews altogether.

The *dokusan* bell is struck twice by the entering student upon hearing the teacher's handbell signaling the end of the previous interview. The student entering the interview room walks to the door of the room and waits for the exiting student to open it. They bow to the teacher together. The entering student enters the room, closes the door, bows again to the teacher, and sits on one's heels in front of the teacher; then, the interview proceeds. The student states his or her name and practice (for example, counting the breath, a particular koan, just sitting); what happens next is not prescribed. Students commonly ask for information about practicing or advice on dealing with problems in practicing, remain silent and listen to the teacher (if the teacher says anything), or demonstrate their understanding that has emerged from their practice. The teacher often responds to the student in the form of talk but also may just ring the bell signaling the end of the interview. The student upon hearing this, bows slightly, stands, opens the door, and does a full bow outside the door with the next entering student, and returns to doing *zazen* in the zendo.

In one of my early interviews with roshi, when I first began doing Zen practice, I entered the room in the prescribed way, told him my name and practice, and began my comments by saying, "I don't know much about Buddhism, but...." He immediately interrupted me and said in a rather kindly way, "I don't know much about Buddh*ism* either. If you want to learn about Buddh*ism,* you should go study with a professor." My experience was one of immediate agreement. Of course, I knew what he meant; that was why I was there instead of in a religious studies class. Having him state it so clearly and frankly had the effect of raising the rapport I felt with him. This was a common experience for me that went well beyond this simple case. What little I knew of his position on marriage and morality, for example, seemed to match my own attitudes. Still, what I was dealing with in the process of my practice (following my breath, doing koans) left me very uncertain and not at all confident in what I was doing. I found him intellectually adept but at the same time not really interested in talking much. I sensed in him someone who knew, who had been there, and not just intellectually. Since in my early days in Zen practice, I tended to understand Zen practice as leading to the sorts of selfless awareness I had experienced while on psychedelic drugs, with the roshi fulfilling the role of one's guide. I particularly valued his guidance. His confidence, clarity, and frankness inspired me and allowed me to immediately accept his authority. The fact that he was the only person to whom I spoke about my practice and, if during a *sesshin,* the only person to whom I spoke at all, reinforced our relationship.

After doing the practice energetically for about seven years, I was working on a koan having to do with a sailboat. After puzzling over it for months, I suddenly grasped its meaning toward the end of a week long *sesshin.* I presented my understanding to him in *dokusan* in a straightforward manner but was not at all sure how he would respond. He looked at me for some time, nodded, and then showed me another way of expressing the same koan. I was again stunned by the fact that he was as intimate with this element of experience as I was, or so it appeared to me at the time. The intimacy of the moment, though entirely unspoken, has never left me. Only in a feverish dream, years earlier, had I felt such intimacy with another. The experience of penetrating to the heart of the koan was significant to me personally. Having the teacher recognize it and be able to show me by his actions that he unambiguously "knew" that same significance (so it seemed) moved my experience beyond the personal into the realm of universal meaning.

Perhaps an explanation of the dream would help clarify what is meant here by intimacy. I had been sick in bed for a few days with a high fever. One night in the midst of this illness I dreamed I was standing near a train that was about to leave a station and there was someone on the train that I dearly yearned for in a very nonspecific way. It was never clear then or now as to the age or sex of this other. The train pulled out of the station, and in my desperation I ran alongside it as it gained speed and threatened to leave me behind. Just as I was about to be left behind, a hand, really only a finger, reached out and for a moment touched my finger as my arm was fully extended in its effort to make contact. In that moment of contact, I felt a completeness of a sort that is not entirely different from the highest form of sexual union known to me, but really much more like the intimacy with the roshi in *dokusan.* More than personal, it points to being in the universal. Some of its power for me certainly had to do with it being a shareable knowing, a reality that was communicable because the other knew it in a similarly immediate fashion. We were not telling each other about it; we were showing each other it (by being it).[2] How does such an account help us to understand the teacher's authority in this setting?

Along these lines Wolff (1976) addresses the possibility of an intersubjective existential truth, which is different from both scientific and everyday (commonsensical) truths in that it recognizes and is based in "an experience of being" (Wolff, 1976, 132–5). What Wolff means by this experience of being approximates what the Zen student (and those who do similar practices) potentially encounter. Wolff notes that this experience has also been called mystical, although he prefers the term "surrender." He finds it directly relevant for doing, or as he puts it, trying sociology.

Wolff's argument for such a truth will not be pursued further here, but it is interesting in that it bears directly on the practices and beliefs that are found in the Zen setting. The issue is not so much theoretical, of course, for Zen students who want to actualize it in their lives, not talk about it. As in the group studied, Wolff sees close contact with a teacher as an essential step in the founding of an intersubjective existential truth.

This third step consists in examining the truth entertained no longer intrasubjectively but in dialogue with another human being. However, for it to be even theoretically possible that the dialogue fulfill its purpose, that is, yield truth, it must be assumed that the partner is *competent* as an examiner or co-examiner, that is, that he, too, has had or can have experiences of being or at any rate can follow reports on them – that he is such a human being, hence that there are such human beings. And in fact, *we hold a relation to one with whom we feel the possibility of such a dialogue, who invites it, or with whom it unexpectedly takes place, to be a particularly personal and important relation:* so close is it to the experience of being itself. (Wolff 1976:129–30; emphasis altered)

He goes on to argue that this relationship can potentially be found with anyone. Here, however, I am concerned with the teacher and how the teacher's authority is experienced by members. Because the teacher has supposedly accomplished what students are trying to accomplish in this regard, this belief and reality, as it is accomplished in interaction with students, are main supports for the teacher's authority and a key ingredient to understanding the vitality of life at the Center.

More practically, the teacher's authority is maintained simply out of the need to maintain a consensus and to avoid the many conflicts of taste and style that are found in any group. The emphasis on seeing a teacher regularly has been used at one group in particular as a social control device for discouraging certain behavior in the zendo by persons doing one or more of the positions mentioned in Chapter II. One of these positions is called the "monitor." Monitors have the job of overseeing the zendo during sitting periods. They sit facing the middle of the room while everyone else sits facing the wall. They watch for persons who might have special needs, such as someone who becomes faint. Sometimes they are also assigned the position of *junko* or of carrying the stick used to encourage those who ask for a stimulating smack on the muscles of the upper back. In some zendos (i.e., under the influence of some particular teachers), the person doing this position also makes encouraging remarks to those sitting from time to time. These remarks are sometimes gentle suggestions like, "Please sit strong," to very vigorous and loud exclamations like, "Wake up!" Whether anything is said at all and just how loudly depends upon the atmosphere the teacher wants to produce and maintain for that particular period of meditation. As mentioned previously, the Rinzai tradition is prone to pushing practitioners in their meditation while the Soto tradition is typically the opposite.

Because Zen practitioners who have been practicing for some years often have experience in various zendos and *sesshins,* and with various teachers, what rules obtain on a particular occasion often is not clear, especially when a group does not have a teacher in residence. In one of the groups studied this ambiguity gave rise to complaints on the part of some beginning students (with the support of some older members) that the "encouraging" remarks of one *junko* were surprising, unsettling, and even frightening. When the senior person in the group was informed of this and suggested to the offender that this encouragement was inappropriate, a disagreement on appropriateness and on who was in charge in the zendo ensued. The disagreement involved for the most part only the person doing the "encouragement" and the senior monk who suggested its suspension. In the absence of a resident teacher, however, or someone who was perceived as a legitimate authority, the result was a standoff and a rule was made that no one can do a position unless they see a teacher at least once a month. When all the concerned parties did so, the difficulty was eliminated. The ritual specialness of this formal occasion of *dokusan,* and members' experiences in doing this interaction with the teacher in the past, increase greatly the likelihood that suggestions or guidance made therein will be taken seriously and as legitimate. Those who do not take such guidance are likely to leave the group, although such cases are rare.

A more complete understanding of authority in this setting depends on the development of a frame of reference that allows agreement at least theoretically on how reality (such as authority) is constructed and maintained. The following incident emphasizes the difficulty of trying to account for authority in terms that do not take into account the unique features of meditative settings.

A student attending *sesshin* came to experience the effects of intensive sitting such as greater relaxation and higher levels of energy available (so much so that in this particular case he had difficulty sleeping). In relating this story to me, the student mentioned that roshi's talks *(teishos)* were very uneven. He noted that sometimes he could not even hear what was said much less understand it. Toward the end of *sesshin,* however, he heard a talk that really affected him. I mentioned to him that it is not uncommon for students to have that sort of experience. More senior members see this as the effects of intensive meditation accumulating over the days, bringing about an alteration in what could be called "normal" consciousness. The ability to concentrate increases drastically and the usual verbal, reflexive processes of thought decrease. One hears differently as this shift occurs. Further, this student was unaware of the distinction made in a Zen context between dharma talks, which are roughly equivalent to sermons, and *teishos,* which frequently make little effort to be discursive. *Teishos* are often said to be manifestations of the teacher's understanding, not a linearly presented communication of it. For those with little practice in doing meditation these *teishos* often make little sense or seem nothing more than the most obvious banalities. For those in the meditative state, however, such talks can be profound in the extreme. This raises the question of meditation and its consequences and how such consequences relate to the production of authority and reality in general in meditative settings. These concerns are addressed in Chapter IV and the topic of authority and special communication between student and teacher is considered in Chapters VII, VIII, and IX.

What is Zen?

The purpose of this chapter is threefold: to outline briefly what Zen is by a description of how and what a prospective member comes to learn about its goals and practices, and how these practices are related to these goals; to describe some basic differences in ways that practitioners are involved in Zen practice; and to develop a view of Zen practice that allows the reader to see it as a particular sort of religious activity that differs considerably from mainline forms of religion. This task involves the use of materials with which Zen practitioners are not always acquainted, but that, nevertheless, are consistent with their experience. This view of Zen, which complements the member's view, will reveal connections between Zen practice as done in the groups studied herein and similar activities in other settings, and reduce the likelihood of misunderstandings by making some definitions and assumptions explicit.

Learning About Zen

Many of those who come to a Zen group have already been exposed to ideas of Zen theory and practice. Over half of those interviewed in this study noted college reading as the source of their first exposure to Zen. The writings of Alan Watts, D. T. Suzuki, and other writers often used in college courses on philosophy and religion had suggested what Zen would be like as a form of religious activity. Others who had not been exposed by means of college reading usually were introduced to Zen by friends or family, the more usual avenue of recruitment to religious groups and social movements in general. People who come to Zen practice, then, have some background information. Especially those who were exposed to the counterculture had clear expectations that Zen would be compatible with their values (Tipton, 1982).

When new members arrive at a Zen group (often called a center) for the first time, they are given instructions on how to meditate and use the meditation hall. These minimal instructions allow them to sit and not disturb others. Those who stay after these first few sittings (and many, perhaps most, do not) are encouraged to do the first available introductory workshop, which usually lasts about six to eight hours. These workshops expose beginners to the basic concepts and practices of Zen. It also provides time for asking questions of a philosophic and ideological nature, which beginners often have. These questions are usually left unanswered, and the questioners are advised not to decide intellectually on the matter but to try doing the practice so they can determine the answers themselves. Beginners come to realize soon enough that the practice is not about beliefs and philosophy.

In the groups studied in this book, the introductory workshops are usually based rather loosely on the lectures of a contemporary Japanese teacher, Yasutani-roshi (d. 1973), which have been published in Kapleau (1967). A wide variety of other sources (spiritual and psychological) are usually synthesized in an informal way by the person giving the workshop. A very brief outline of the topics of these lectures, freely interpreted, is: All living beings are Buddhas (i.e., enlightened), but they fail to see this. *Zazen* (sitting meditation) is the practical demonstration of this theory. Other Buddhist teachings are important but are not a prerequisite to practice. Finally, we need to wake up our true nature (self).

This outline emphasizes two basic "givens" of Zen: First, we are all inherently enlightened, and second, we need to practice *zazen* to realize and actualize this enlightenment (defined as seeing into one's "true nature") in our daily lives. These two assumptions/realities produce a continual tension in Zen practice and discourse between the two notions of *zazen* as training for enlightenment, and *zazen* as the manifestation of one's already enlightened state. The saying, "We sit because we are enlightened, not to become enlightened," exemplifies this tension while putting emphasis on the second point. This saying, however, should not be taken to mean that Zen training is not a skillful means to realizing enlightenment. In fact, an analogy is often used in introductory talks to make this view clear. The "Mind" (used in contrast to ego awareness) is like a mountain lake that reflects the moon. Usually the lake is so disturbed by the waves of everyday thinking and emotions that one cannot see the moon's reflection. *Zazen* is the practice of stilling those waves so that one's true nature can be seen clearly reflected on it. Zen is said to be less a particular set of beliefs than a finger pointing to the moon, or a ladder one uses to accomplish a task, which is then thrown away after the task is accomplished. This special use of language, characteristic of Zen discourse (both formal and informal), is not easily accepted by new members. It tends to have the very practical consequence of stopping conversation and the "normal" (i.e., reflexive) effort to understand what is going on and to fit it into commonsense categories.

Zen tends to share many of its assumptions and teachings with other meditative traditions.

Monistic groups assert a social unity hidden in the depths of the self. They posit a universal Self immanent in particular selves, by which individuals are harmoniously related to each other and to nature. Such hidden interconnections between people are not dependent upon consciously shared religious or political values.

Within most monistic systems, consciously shared value frameworks are considered intrinsically illusory. According to such perspectives, rational theologies and political ideologies are based upon distinctions between logically opposed categories of experience. Such discursive ordering of experience is seen as intrinsically illusory in that it is arbitrary and culturally relative. An indefinite number of such orderings is possible, and therefore, no one system is more correct than any other. According to monists, belief in a particular rational ordering of experience is the essence of Maya – the illusory world of opposites. *Real knowledge involves the faculty of perception, not that of reason.* (Robbins & Anthony, 1981, 21; emphasis added)

This commitment to knowledge lying in altered perception rather than discursive thought processes is a key constitutive element of Zen experience and meditation-based insight in general (Tart, 1975, 94). Intuition replaces step-by-step, consciously based knowledge-production processes; however, intuition is not less rational, only less incremental and discursive. Eliade (1969, 73) makes this point in differentiating one form of meditation from both poetic imagination and Bergonsian intuition: "What sharply distinguishes yogic meditation from these two irrational 'flights' is its coherence, the state of lucidity that accompanies and continually orients it."

What the term enlightenment (*kensho* is the Japanese term preferred in the groups studied) means in the Zen context is a very complex question. In the view of one contemporary scholar, it is an experience that can vary in form from very primitive experiences of transcendence to the profound insight manifested in the teachings associated with the names of the Buddha, Christ, Krishna, and Lao-Tzu (Wilber, 1981, 251). As the term is more commonly used, it refers to an experience, sometimes called the mystical experience, or ecstasy (Laski 1961) in which the normal limits of self and knowing are transcended. They are characterized according to James (1903) as being ineffable, involving not just feeling but knowing as well, of a transitory nature, and dependent upon a state of "passivity" – that is, they cannot be simply willed. Of the large literature on this topic, perhaps the most helpful is that of transpersonal psychology,

The Los Angeles meditation hall (zendo). Notice the altar at the right.

which synthesizes the rich classical literature of the world religions with contemporary psychological interests and perspectives. For Zen practitioners, however, and for our purposes, we can consider enlightenment experiences to be highly desirable, if rare, events in an individual's life. The role that they play in Zen practice will be seen more clearly.[1]

Because Zen meditation *(zazen)* is the practical demonstration (in Yasutani's terms) of Buddhist philosophy, the introductory lectures turn to it directly. The emphasis is on how it is done. The student is told that through meditation you will have these experiences that have been referred to theoretically. Only by trying it will you see if it is true, a recommendation common in various groups (Stone 1978). To do *zazen* the beginner is instructed to find a quiet, comfortable spot (if not in the zendo), find a cushion of appropriate size to sit on, wear loose-fitting clothes, sit in a proper posture (of various sorts) with the buttocks on the cushion, holding the spine straight, the hands together about belt level, eyes down at about a forty-five degree angle; then, looking at a point about three feet in front, relax the muscles across the shoulders, breathe normally, and attend to what the teacher has assigned as one's practice.

Beginners are usually assigned the practice of counting the breath, that is, inhalations and exhalations from one to ten and then starting over again at one. As this practice is mastered, one is asked to follow the breath without guiding or counting it. After beginning students progress this far, and it often takes months of practice (if not more) to do it well, they are often started on koan study. Koans are riddles or puzzles that do not have intellectual solutions. They have the practical consequence of exhausting the usual discursive and reflexive techniques used to solve problems and produce commonsense experience while bringing the practitioner to a state of extreme tension and, potentially, openness to insight. Regardless of what practice one is doing, all forms of practice tend to produce a slowing or stopping of normal, commonsense processes of reality construction.[2]

Another point in which beginners are often instructed is the importance of that part of the body that the Japanese call *hara* (cf. Lebra, 1976, 159–63). This body/spiritual center is noted as the center of gravity of the body, as an energy center, and as the point where attention should be directed during meditative practices. The notion of "contemplating one's navel" is a facetious statement of the location of this center (which actually lies an inch or so below the navel) that belies its important role in a variety of practices in Asia, including the martial arts (cf. von Duerckheim, 1977). The student finds that one needs regular reminders and corrections to get the basics of sitting and practice right before beginning to achieve the meditative state. A great deal of time is spent during later talks, reminding students of how to do *zazen* properly so to be able to begin to concentrate the mind.

Varieties of Zen Practice

Because students come to Zen with different goals or needs, there are various practitioners and forms of practice. Yasutani (1967) speaks of this as the five varieties of *zazen*. Usually only a couple of varieties are mentioned in the introductory workshops but because they help us to identify some sociologically interesting differences among members, we will examine them in a more detail here.

Ordinary Zen

Ordinary *zazen* is entirely secular, without any religious notions, and is done in the belief that it can reduce stress and improve health in general. This form of practice is undertaken by many newcomers to Zen. Yasutani notes that this form of practice "is bound to eliminate sickness of a psychosomatic nature" (Kapleau, 1967, 42), although the groups studied for this report are careful to recommend that prospective members with severe emotional problems seek professional therapeutic help.[3]

These practitioners, then, are recognizable, yet diverse. They initially take a highly instrumental approach to the practice and, if they stay on this level of practice, are unable, according to Yasutani, to break through the dualism of self and world. One practitioner who views his beginning to do Zen practice as the result of a divorce, a sudden illness, and abuse of drugs, realized he needed to do something and he notes:

Yogic practice seemed kind of harebrained, magical. I wasn't very interested in magic. I was more interested in some practical way to solve my difficulties. (no. 32, 2)

This person later became a resident of the Los Angeles Center and a monk. Another practitioner commented:

What really began to get me sitting was I (pause) I'm a compulsive ... [word omitted to preserve anonymity] and it is a tremendous problem for me. So I started to work with a program like AA and part of the thing with this is, just like AA, it involves an acceptance of a power higher than yourself. That immediately brought me back to my concept of god and my lost Christian faith. I couldn't go back that route but I wanted to work the program because I needed it. So I made Zen my higher power and began doing Zen practice regularly. (paraphrased from no. 58, 2)

A contemporary Zen teacher may have this group of practitioners in mind when he writes:

Without religious devotion, Zen becomes a kind of hobby. Without the great death and great rebirth, it becomes a kind of self improvement exercise. It is not a subject to be mastered with a certain form or a certain curriculum, but a lifetime training. (Aitken, 1976, xiii)

Non-Buddhist Religious Zen

This form is done on the basis of other religious beliefs and principles. We find many Catholics who undertake Zen practice as a form of prayer, and surprisingly enough there is at present a Jesuit priest who is also a Zen teacher. Thomas Merton (1968) represents this variety of Zen admirably. Yasutani notes that those seeking occult "powers" of clairvoyance or action at a distance are also to be considered in this variety. Relatively few practitioners in the groups studied are of this sort, however. We might also include in this latter category those persons with psychedelic experience who had encountered some form of "religious" experience and who seek enlightenment but have non-Buddhist notions of what this would be like.

A senior monk notes of his early interest in Zen practice:

I read *Three Pillars of Zen.* It sounded very enticing. In fact, at that time I regularly consumed drugs of various kinds and it seemed like a wonderful way to get high without having to take drugs. (no. 29, 1)

Peak experiences of whatever origins (not necessarily drug induced), encountered before beginning Zen practice, present the practitioner with expectations that are not always congruent with the Buddhist idiom. One practitioner says of an experience he had before beginning Zen practice:

It was a very powerful experience. At a certain level it really made a believer out of me as to the existence of those levels of consciousness ... in a way that was more than intellectual. At that time, with that experience, it made it real for me in a total sort of way.... I later came to refer to it as a kind of satori experience. At the time I wasn't able to talk about it in terms of Zen. (no. 62, 1)

The Zen of the Lesser Buddhist Way

In this form of practice, the individual, according to Yasutani, strives for a strictly personal enlightenment. This form of *zazen* is "an expedient Zen for those unable to grasp the innermost meaning of the Buddha's enlightenment ... that we cannot attain genuine peace of mind merely by seeking our own salvation while remaining indifferent to the welfare of others" (Kapleau, 1967, 44). This (Hinayana Buddhist) form might well be the most commonly practiced, knowingly or not, by American practitioners, whose exposure to the American ideology of individualism and lack of intimacy with the Buddhist frame of reference make it quite attractive.[4]

The Zen of the Greater Buddhist Way

"This is a truly Buddhist Zen, for it has as its central purpose ... seeing into your essential nature and realizing the Way in your daily life" (Kapleau, 1967, 45). *Zazen* is practiced with the goal of experiencing enlightenment in a profound experience of *kensho.* Perhaps a majority of practitioners who actually live in the Zen community studied in Los Angeles would fall into this category. They are doing some form of koan study and are relatively well-informed and committed Buddhists. They differ from that style of practice outlined as "the lesser way" by understanding their practice in terms of "service to others" – a commonly emphasized theme in the groups studied. This form of practice is closely tied to the Mahayana form of Buddhism.

A Fifth Form of Zen

Yasutani notes a fifth form of *zazen* involving the practice of "just sitting" where *zazen* is done not as a means to an end but as a manifestation of the enlightened state itself. One has faith that enlightenment will occur without striving for it self-consciously. Relatively few do this practice in the groups studied.

What do these five types of Zen practice suggest about the meaning of Zen? In one sense they indicate five different meanings that members hold. This notion of meaning is defined by Schutz:

Our problem ... is not what occurs to man as a psycho-physiological unit, but the attitude he adopts toward these occurrences – briefly, the *subjective meaning* man bestows upon certain experiences of his own spontaneous life. (Schutz, 1967, 210; emphasis added)

For Schutz, then, meaning involves reflecting on experience that relates the particular experiences to a purpose or goal. As the goal, in this case, of Zen practice differs, its subjective meaning also differs.

One meaning of Zen practice and experiences associated therewith is that it leads to enlightenment. Enlightenment is a theoretical term, albeit one that is, according to Buddhists, capable of being grounded in experience beyond mere conceptual thought. It is used by some members to make sense of their involvement in Zen practice. Enlightenment becomes the goal, so to speak, of some of the practices, and these practices take their meaning, on a very elementary level, from their relationship to this ultimate project. Not all practitioners pursue enlightenment, however, although others have goals and purposes that are used in a similar way to shape the meaning of their participation in Zen practice. This approach allows a person doing Zen practice to improve one's health or to gain occult powers, for example, to understand what one is doing in purely secular terms. The rituals, robes, and bells of Zen might look like religion to some, but to this sort of practitioner, they are merely the elements of a technique for producing very practical, not at all "religious" results. Catholics (or participants in any other religious form), on the other hand, can do Zen practice and maintain its meaning as entirely consistent with their particular commitments and teachings. Thus, we find various types of Zen practitioners who define the meaning of Zen practice in various ways.

This scheme of varieties of *zazen* recognizes that different persons are at different times in their lives willing and able to do different sorts of practice. Teachers emphasize matching the practice to the individual, and information from the individual practitioner as well as the judgment of the teacher are needed to decide on the proper practice for a person at a particular time. As one matures in the practice, it is usual for the form of one's involvement to move in the direction of the higher numbered variety.

Regardless of which form of *zazen* is done, however, all tend to produce an increase in the ability to concentrate. To the extent that any practice produces an increase in the power to concentrate, then, it might be said to have an element of "Zen" to it. But Yasutani sees two other aims of *zazen* that go beyond just raising this power of concentration: satori-awakening or the experiencing of a profound insight into the nature of reality from the Zen point of view (a mystical experience from a more general viewpoint); and the actualization of the supreme way in our daily lives. The following elements, then, are the aims or goals of *zazen:* increasing concentration, having an enlightenment experience, and making the experience of enlightenment a part of everyday life.

In addition, the introductory talks usually have some helpful information on how to meet behavioral requirements in the meditation hall – what to do during service, interviews with the teacher, and so on.[5] The beginner, even after the workshop, is still quite uncertain of what "Zen" is. This introductory lesson is so superficial or so difficult to appreciate at first that for practical purposes the beginner gets very little solid information. One gets some advice about what Zen is not and how not to think about it, but, more than anything else, one gets advice on how to do Zen meditation.

This neglect of "theory" and beliefs is no accident. Not only does Zen not stress believing, one is even discouraged from asking questions of a philosophic or theological nature. Let those questions go and just do the meditation practices and deal with what occurs, one is told, and these questions will be resolved. The substance of the matter of Zen is in *zazen* practice. Rather than thinking or believing, experience is the key. Yet Zen is not anti-intellectual. In fact, the group studied has the reputation of being one of the more intellectually involved Zen groups in the United States. Technical thought is considered fine. The inappropriate use of thought that interferes with living an enlightened life is what Zen warns against.

If the reader is left with a feeling of uneasiness concerning what Zen is really about and with questions about the meaning of terms like enlightenment or concentration, this is just the position the beginner is in. Except the beginner now is guided to do sitting meditation and other practices that ground the introductory talks in experience. The third task of this chapter is to place Zen in a context of social scientific discourse that will help conceive of Zen practice as a social phenomenon.

Zen Viewed Sociologically

Some concerns are not explicitly taught in introductory talks (or in other talks, for that matter). One of these considers the overall career of the serious Zen practitioner. No effort is made to describe this path because knowing it does not really give one anything except perhaps another set of ideas to distract one's practice. Even though very few remarks are made about stages or steps in Zen practice and, with the exception of seating in the zendo and service positions, little effort is made to differentiate a hierarchy of accomplishment among the community of practitioners, there is still implicit in these talks and in the organization of the practice a sense of long-term career of one who does the practice successfully. This last section deals with such dimensions of the Zen setting, which are largely implicit in members' experience.

A Zen practitioner himself, Wilber (1983) provides a statement that allows an understanding of what the beginner is faced with in coming to deal with Zen, as well as an understanding of some of the implicit realities of Zen practice. One of these involves a distinction between belief, faith, and experience. Because they often deal with religion in terms of its social functions (e.g., as a meaning system), sociologists have often found belief to be the most interesting feature of religion. In fact, Wilber argues,

belief is the lowest form of religious involvement, and ... it often seems to operate with no authentic religious connection whatsoever. The "true believer" – one who has no literal faith, let alone actual experience – embraces a more-or-less codified belief system that appears to act most basically as a fund of immortality symbols. (Wilber, 1983, 65)

He notes that beliefs function differently on different levels of religious sensitivity, but they still remain less than essential for getting at what Zen, for example, is about.

Wilber deals with faith as separate from belief. He argues that "the person of faith tends to shun literalism, dogmatism, evangelicalism, fundamentalism, which define almost solely the true believer" (1983, 67). Unlike the true believer, faith is often accompanied by doubt. This is recognized in the saying: great doubt, great enlightenment; small doubt, small enlightenment; no doubt, no enlightenment.

In the case of Zen, then, faith is important but in the viewpoint of the present study, it is not sufficient to understand how the phenomenon is constituted.[6] One moves on immediately by means of the practice to experience. In fact, some might say that Zen begins with experience. As noted previously there is a form of Zen practice that is totally secular, independent of any "religious" faith at all. Regardless of the practitioner's faith or belief or form of practice, the crucial element is encountering the experience that is, in a sense, the practical result of cognitive claims, beliefs, and commitments. The roshi in the Los Angeles group speaks to this point.

Mere physical sitting is not enough. You have to sit carefully and attentively. Let your body sit, let your blood circulation sit. Let everything sit. Then your sitting becomes indestructible, immovable. And when you really penetrate into it, it becomes more than that: the entire world in ten directions becomes one bright jewel. Nothing to move and nothing to be moved.... That's zazen. As Master Dogen mentions, don't just understand it conceptually, but understand it with your whole body and mind. When you practice in this way, your zazen becomes nothing but the unshakable, indestructible, enlightened state itself. Extending that practice into everyday life, your whole life becomes the enlightened life.[7]

Far from being an emotional frenzy or trance, this experience resembles what Maslow has called a peak experience. An authentic religious (in contrast to trance) experience then is one that "can be blissful, but it is also numinous, noetic, illuminative, and – most importantly – it carries a great deal more insight or understanding" (Wilber, 1983, 69). This experience is what the introductory talks refer to as enlightenment, *ken-sho* or *satori* (a word not preferred in the groups studied), and it is understood in terms very similar to Wilber's.[8]

Looking beyond Wilber for a more social scientific frame of reference for dealing with religious experience presents a problem, however, in that it is relatively neglected as a topic. Conversion is studied extensively, of course, but religious experience, when treated at all, is usually taken as "feeling states" and in the view of one writer, the analysis is carried "to the point of vivisection, losing the essential quality of the living experience" (Straus, 1981, 59). Three recent studies that do take religious experience seriously and sympathetically attempt its analysis are Boyle (1984), Ellwood (1980), and Straus (1981). These works begin the development of a theoretical statement of how such experiences can be studied by sociology.

My interest in Zen, however, is not limited to the study of profound religious experience; in fact so-called enlightenment experiences are hardly considered in this study. My primary concern is with the transformation in the experience of reality that a practitioner can undergo in the process of doing Zen practice or Zen training. In other words, it is the whole process of "conversion" that is the topic of interest, not just profound experiences. This wider concern with how experience of reality is collectively produced and shared makes social theory in general, not just that exclusively devoted to religious topics, useful for my purposes.

Besides using the literature on conversion and commitment (reviewed briefly in Chapter V), the analysis of Zen in this study draws on three sources of social theory that have in common an interest in what can loosely be called the "sociology of the body." This term suggests a concern with the body, emotions, and bodily energies in general; how these energies are modulated and shared with others in the processes of ritual interactions; and how the body (not just the mind) figures in the production of social phenomena. The three main sources of theory used are:

1. the Durkheim/Goffman/Collins school that provides a theory of ritual interaction that details the importance of ritual and bodily energies for the production of experience and agreement on its meaning (see Chapters VIII and IX).

2. the work of Sudnow, especially *Ways of the Hand,* provides a convincing description of the role of the body and the reduced role of intentionality in the process of doing jazz improvisation (see Chapter VII).

3. Bourdieu's use of the term "habitus" in his *Outline of a Theory of Practice,* which argues the importance of subjectively shared dispositions for social action and links them to a notion of "practice" (see Chapter VIII). We take advantage of these efforts, as well as the unpretentious scheme found in introductory Zen talks, to guide us in a study of how Zen experience is related to the particular activities found in Zen settings. This leads to an examination not of "Zen" but of Zen Practice.

Zen Practice

What is Zen? The question is rarely asked by practitioners themselves for various reasons, but it is commonly asked by beginners. Teachers are known to say something like, "Zen is life," or "Zen is nothing special," or "Zen is not separate from ordinary mind," and then they pass on immediately to those points of Yasutani's lectures noted previously: We are already enlightened, we do not see it, we need to practice to see it, so how do we practice? The question is turned around to direct attention to how the meaning of Zen is to be encountered and actualized in everyday life. It is repeatedly pointed out that talking about it cannot adequately express it. One needs to do the practice of meditation oneself to see what it means. It is in the doing (or as we will see, in the not doing) of it that the meaning of "Zen" is revealed.

Often there is no clear distinction made between Zen meditation and Zen practice. One commonly hears the expression, "How to sit (i.e., do *zazen*) is how to live." Usually, however, meditation means *zazen*, whereas practice refers not just to *zazen* but to a wide variety of both formally ritualized (seeing a teacher regularly in interviews, for example) and other less formalized activities (earning a living, for example). A senior Zen student reports:

When I first began doing Zen practice I thought that it was the special postures and focus of attention that I associated with *zazen*. The more I practiced, however, the more I extended my mindful attitude to other activities so that now there is no part of my life that isn't available to me as an occasion for practice. The puzzling result of this is that "Zen" as something special has disappeared and I'm left with just my life the way it is moment after moment. (Paraphrased from no. 33, 1985)

What exactly does the word "practice" mean and how can it be studied as a social phenomenon? It occurs repeatedly when practitioners talk with one another but its meaning is not so easily stated. A senior monk notes:

You don't even need to call it Buddhism or Zen or *zazen* or practice. You can call it learning or, ah, ah, what would you call it? All these names put up a big wall, they get a reaction. It's learning to be human, I think. (no. 33, 13)

One common meaning of practice that is associated with religious settings is a set of customary or habitual activities that include forms of prayer, work, and service. This meaning usually includes no notion of practice as techniques for realizing spiritual development; instead, the emphasis is on such practices as mere traditional ways of life. Some even see them as cultural anachronisms that people turn to in their search for meaning. Another common meaning of practice is the exercise or pursuit of a profession or occupation. A more helpful common meaning is that of repeated performance or systematic exercise for the purpose of acquiring skill or proficiency. Although this definition too falls short of what practice involves in a Zen setting, it provides a basis on which a clearer theoretical statement can be made. Rather than develop this theoretical statement of Zen practice here, however, it is deferred (see Chapter VIII) until after the alternative approaches to the study of "conversion" and their limitations in a Zen setting are discussed.[9]

CHAPTER V

Meditation as a Social Phenomenon: I

Meditation viewed as a social phenomenon[1] is perhaps most easily discussed with the issues of so-called conversion and commitment to a religious group. These issues in turn are part of a complex of assumptions and concepts that make up the various theories of socialization in general, or how one becomes a member of any group, religious or secular. While conversion is a popular topic for sociologists to study, especially in the last decade or so (see Heirich, 1977; Lofland & Skonovd, 1981; Long & Hadden, 1983; and Robbins, Anthony, & Richardson, 1978; for summaries of this literature), the sociological literature on meditation is very small indeed. Chapters V and VI examine meditation as a social phenomenon by considering and then criticizing two main theories of conversion and commitment: social learning theory in the form of symbolic interactionism, and a popular variety of phenomenological sociology generally associated with the "lifeworld" *(Lebenswelt)* view of Schutz (1967). These views of conversion and commitment are helpful, but they need be complemented by a view that takes meditative practices seriously and sees them as significantly different from received notions of what occurs in conversion settings. On the basis of this examination and critique, we will develop an alternative view of conversion processes in meditative settings. This view of meditation provides a scheme that is elaborated in Chapters VII, VIII, and IX.

Becoming a Zen Practitioner

What are the actual processes or conditions involved in converting to a religious group and increasing one's commitment to it? One influential model is that of Lofland and Stark (1965), which treats conversion and commitment as a process of becoming deviant. Lofland (1966) used this in his study of the early Unification Church. Other groups that use a similarly skeptical approach to new religious forms are those interested in the potentially dangerous and coercive aspects of cultlike groups. While there is a sizable literature using the perspective of coercive persuasion, perhaps the most extreme is Conway and Siegelman (1978), who argue that in joining nearly all new religious groups, even quasi-religious groups such as est (Erhard Seminars Training), there is a drastic psychological transformation made under conditions similar to brainwashing.

Conceptualizing new religious activity as deviance or as a form of brainwashing is criticized by Balch (1980) and Balch and Taylor (1977), who see this perspective as not adequate to explain their experience with members of a UFO cult. Instead they find a cultic milieu or metaphysical subculture that allows us to see the joining of these groups as desirable, commendable, and as a supported activity by others within that subculture. Rather than deviant, they argue conversion and commitment can be studied as a normal process of role learning.

Among the various approaches to the study of conversion, structural studies attempt to specify the conditions that predispose persons to become seekers and joiners of new religious forms. A typical assumption is that the joiners are passive in the face of conditions that cause them to take up the new behavior and join the new group. Conditions such as marginality and stress are seen as predisposing them to new religious activity. Another group of sociologists emphasize situational factors (Gerlach & Hine, 1970). Here emphasis is put not on the causes of participation, but on how the person actually goes about accomplishing the conversion to the reality of the new group (Damrell 1977; Lofland 1977; Straus 1979). A number of studies of conversion and commitment in several groups have used both structural and situational features (see Robbins, Anthony, & Richardson, 1978). They have typically criticized the Lofland and the Gerlach and Hine models for being only partially adequate to their particular research settings. Lofland (1977), in reviewing this literature, suggests one would be better advised to report what is seen in a particular group rather than taking his and Stark's model as basic. This chapter attempts to do just that.

Between the alarmist posture of Conway and Siegelman and the more rationalist position of role learning, there is a way of dealing with the processes of learning a new religious activity that gives the individual considerably more freedom and responsibility for making sense of one's own activity. Following Lofland (1977) and Straus (1979), I treat a form of learning a new religious practice as a process of experimental learning with considerable individual variation and effort involved. The beginning stages of becoming a Zen practitioner can be treated the way Becker

(1953) treated how one learns to use marijuana. Certain aspects of the processes of learning how to use marijuana for pleasure and of becoming a Zen practitioner are nearly identical. Two commonalities of these processes are that they are entered voluntarily, and, in contrast to assumptions commonly made of cults exerting intense social pressure to convert, participants eagerly seek the experience they believe is available to insiders. This analysis sheds light on the learning of a new religious activity and how it is actually accomplished by the individual.

Of course, I do not intend to detract in any way from Zen practice as a bona fide spiritual activity. D. T. Suzuki, in criticizing G. B. Sansom's efforts to address Zen and its role in Japanese history, points out that it is extremely difficult if not impossible for Western categories of thought to grasp Zen adequately (see Sansom, 1978, 349–50). I make no effort to do this whatsoever. On the contrary, this chapter deals with certain mundane aspects of Zen practice that allow the beginner to come to participate in the activity of Zen. It has been suggested that the experience of *zazen* is a fact that needs no interpretation, just as the taste of tea is the same for everyone.[2] There is no philosophy necessarily attached to sitting, and thus Catholics, or persons of any other religion, can do *zazen* without giving up their own beliefs (and, as we have noted, some do). In the groups studied, for example, rabbis and Catholic nuns and priests often participate. It is possible to experience *zazen* and then to understand the meaning of the experience in terms of the language and beliefs of one's own particular religion. The focus is on an activity, the objectified meaning of which, and the learning of which, can be dealt with by the sociologist without denying in any way its broader implications or validity.

Zen Buddhism is usually treated by sociologists as one of the new religions in the United States today (Bird, 1978; Glock & Bellah, 1976; Tipton, 1979). Zen has been practiced for some time in the West, but it has experienced a new vigor, along with other new religious forms, in the last decade or two. In contrast to many new religious groups, Zen groups in the United States are not totally involving. They usually encourage even the individual who lives in a communal Zen setting to continue commitments to family, community, and occupation. In this respect Zen groups are more like the Pentecostal group studied by Harrison (1974) than the more demanding and involving cultlike movements that have received more attention from sociologists (cf. Bromley & Shupe, 1979). In a further contrast with many new religious groups, which are often successfully labeled deviant, Zen is seen by many as a respectable activity. This perception no doubt stems from its association with the upper class in Japan and with high cultural activities in general, but also from the social characteristics of the members themselves (see Chapter II).

Consequences of Meditative Practice

In trying to use the standard models of conversion and commitment to account for becoming a Zen practitioner, I have found them only partially adequate. First, they tend to miss the more subtle dimensions of conversion experience.[3] Second, and more important for the purposes of this chapter, they do not deal with the physiological impact and symptoms of meditation and thus miss an important aspect of learning to become a member. Physiological symptoms of religious experience have been treated by Frank (1961) and Sargant (1957), psychotherapists who have seen similarities between what occurs in religious experiences and in successful psychotherapy and brainwashing. For them the common denominator is a drastic interruption of normal brain functioning. But by limiting physiological changes to drastic and unusual experiences of conversion, "baptism of the spirit" and similar events, they have inadvertently obscured the presence and the role of more common physiological consequences. Even Gerlach and Hine (1970), who admit the reality of physiological consequences, speak only of general "cognitive consequences" and limit these also to the powerful experiences of "baptism." In the case of Zen, there are physiological consequences that are common and spread over one's career of participation in the practice and are not limited to drastic and powerful experiences. Learning is thus a continuing process in which the consequences are regularly encountered by even the isolated practitioner.

Because *zazen* is a practice that in many ways can be related to other kinds of meditation from other traditions, some of my comments can be generalized to other forms of meditation. The point is that the sitting meditation learned by Zen practitioners produces consequences of various sorts, the most objectively obvious of which are physiological. As will be seen in Chapter VI, changes in pulse rate, depth and rate of breathing, brain wave patterns, and so on have been measured by researchers interested in just such a connection. More important for our purposes, sitting has consequences that are analogous to the consequences of smoking marijuana or taking a mind-altering drug like LSD. There is no need to argue that they are identical or that these are the only consequences of meditation, just that there is an analogous relationship. Both practices, marijuana smoking and doing *zazen,* effectively produce consequences of a psychological–physiological nature. Consequently, the logic of Becker's (1953) analysis of the process of learning to use marijuana for pleasure is applicable to the process of learning to become a Zen practitioner. Focusing on how beginners deal with physiological consequences of sitting provides a somewhat different perspective on the processes of conversion and commitment.

Becker's Model

Becker presents a model of marijuana use that disagrees with so-called predispositional theories, which assume that drug use is to be understood in terms of conditions and experiences that occur before an individual's actual contact with the drug. In contrast to this, Becker focuses on the changes in attitude and experience an individual has in the process of learning how to smoke marijuana and the resulting symptoms, how one comes to recognize the symptoms and attach them to the use of the drug, and finally how one defines these experiences as pleasurable (Becker, 1953). There is work done by the person in learning the meaning of his or her experience as pleasure.

In the case of the beginning Zen student, learning to do sitting meditation involves similar changes in attitude and experience. By tracing the process of how one learns to sit properly so as to produce the symptoms, recognize the symptoms as a product of sitting, and assign them meaning that allows one to take encouragement from them, we can learn about how beginning Zen practice is accomplished.

What follows is a typical analysis of a typical participant and does not deny the possibility of gifted persons who are drawn to such a practice and experience its more profound dimensions immediately. Our present concern is the learning an individual does in relating the more common and mundane experiences of sitting meditation to the goal of enlightenment (or whatever an individual's goal happens to be).

This section follows closely the line of argument in Becker's article. He begins his analysis with a person who is willing to try marijuana. This person knows others use it to "get high," is curious about its consequences, but is somewhat afraid of the experience. Taking the following three steps leaves one willing and able to use marijuana for pleasure. It is a learning process that can be interrupted or stopped at any point (Becker 1953).

Learning to Produce the Symptoms

The novice marijuana smoker does not ordinarily get high the first time. People account for this inability to get high in terms of not using the drug properly. What is needed is some technique for getting enough marijuana into the lungs and the blood stream so that the symptoms can be experienced (Becker, 1953).

This applies directly to Zen practitioners in the early stages. Because there is really no aggressive program to recruit new members, people have to come when they are curious and willing to try it. In the trying of the sitting meditation, people often report they do not experience the

A meditation period during a *sesshin* at the old zendo in San Diego. More commonly, participants sit facing the walls.

"symptoms" the first time. Technique is emphasized in introducing the beginner to sitting. Introductory talks and constant guidance throughout, not just in the beginning, provide information on how to sit properly so as to accomplish the effects. This information is available from some books, from teachers, or from others already in the practice. Part of the technique involves sitting still, usually in some variety of a cross-legged position, keeping the spine straight and the eyes open but not looking around, with attention on, say, one's breathing. As is usually explained to the beginner, this procedure allows the stilling of the mind and a gradual diminution of the distorting waves of everyday consciousness.

This technique seems to encourage a modality of being in the world that is grounded in the body, which has physiological–psychological states (calming of the mind, reduction of physical stress) that allow the person to attend to experiences that one perhaps had been too busy, too confused, or too culture-bound to consider before. It allows movement into a state of physical being that has a concomitant mind state with the potential for new insights and learning. That it is a process of "deconditioning" is a common understanding of the practitioners themselves.

So we see already at this stage that, contrary to some notions about joining new religious groups, learning to be a Zen practitioner is not taking on a new set of beliefs; it is not memorizing a philosophy; and it is certainly not group-focused and intense interaction in the usual sense of these terms. It is quite similar to smoking marijuana. Do it correctly or miss it completely. Interestingly, in the groups studied, a large proportion of those who subsequently dropped out of Zen reported severe leg pain, which interfered with their successful sitting. Sitting might be seen, then, as a body-based form of phenomenological "bracketing" (see Chapter VI) – a way of seeing into the self and the taken-for-granted realities of everyday life.

Recognizing the Symptoms

Even using proper technique a person may not get high. According to Becker, the user must consciously connect symptoms with having smoked; otherwise, regardless of the actual effects, the user assumes there were no effects. Such persons believe the whole thing an illusion and self-deception on the part of a user who does get high. Typically, the novice has faith, based on observation of those who get high, that the drug will produce some new experience and continues to experiment until it does. The novice is eager to experience and learns new concepts from others that make it possible to identify something different that can be connected with drug use. Only when one can do this is one said to "get high." And only when one gets high will one continue to use the drug for pleasure. If one loses the ability to perceive effects, then marijuana use ceases (Becker, 1953).

There is tremendous incentive to stop sitting immediately. Doing it successfully or otherwise, one is impressed by leg pain and the frustration of sitting without moving for a half-hour at a time. These difficulties no doubt discourage any "romantic" notions that may have motivated a person to begin sitting. In contrast to some other new religious forms, and especially the "human potential movement" (Stone, 1976), Zen seems to have few "beautiful people" who are along for the fun of it. Although those members interviewed almost unanimously saw "all kinds of people" doing Zen practice, it was generally agreed that they tended to be more serious than usual and more disappointed with the standard roles and rewards of American society. Further, there is relatively little socializing going on in the early stages. In fact, compared with the time spent sitting, and the intensity of this time, socializing is slight and not sufficient cause for continuing in the practice. It is not unusual for beginners especially to avoid much socializing with other Zen members and to prefer to limit contact to the formal activity of sitting. As one person remembered of his early experience:

I didn't want to have a bunch of people coming over and talk to me a lot. I just wanted to have them give me the space to sit. (no. 3)

Thus unless one can recognize the symptoms of sitting, there are many reasons to discontinue this difficult practice, just as Becker (and the logic of the social learning perspective) suggests.

Some common consequences of sitting that are reported by practitioners include: a reduction of anxiety and an increase in relaxation with a concomitant change in pulse and breath rates; a recognition of things going on in one's body; a realization that time is not always linear so that it collapses or drags interminably; the experience of images, feelings, and emotions that may range from very enjoyable to very frightening; and a gradual ability to concentrate better. One student of Zen writes of his early experience:

Every one of my allergies has disappeared, my stomach pains me only occasionally, I sleep well. . . . The dark fears which formerly haunted me, my cherished dreams and hopes, all these have withered away, leaving me with a clearer sense of the real. (Kapleau, 1965, 224)

In discussions with others, interviews with a teacher, and similar activities, a student learns to identify these and other experiences as symptoms of sitting meditation but not necessarily the goals of it. The concept of *makyo* ("mysterious vision") is a general term used in the group studied to refer to intense feelings, images, and so forth that are commonly reported by beginners when getting into deep meditation for the first time. This notion allows beginners to locate and label something different in their experience. At this point sitters might be said to be "high" in Becker's sense in that they can recognize experience as produced by sitting.

Assigning Meaning to the Symptoms

Returning to Becker, the user must learn to enjoy the effects of the drug one has learned to experience. A naive interpretation of the effects may well be confusing unless it can be defined as pleasurable. Interaction with more experienced users provides this definition (Becker, 1953).

It would not be correct to say Zen practitioners sit for pleasure, even though they report that considerable relaxation and refreshment seem to follow from it. The commonly stated goal is to forget the self and attain enlightenment. We have already seen that many experiences of the beginner come to be dismissed by the teacher as, "The best are useless and the worst are harmless."

What is the equivalent of enjoyment in Becker's third step? The ultimate goal of enlightenment is appealing, certainly, but practically, day in and day out, when staying in bed seems more appealing than enlightenment, how does one get out of bed and down on the cushion? Although practitioners have different motivations and levels of accomplishment, the experience of disappointment with life and even desperation in the search for peace of mind is very commonly reported. Roughly half of those interviewed linked their beginning Zen practice to a crisis in their life. This desperation, especially among beginners, helps account for continued participation. Zen is generally recognized as a difficult path and those drawn to it report it is attractive just because it is "practical" and "effective." Others used the words "direct," "concrete," and "grounded." The emphasis is on experience, not belief; it is not for pleasure but for the realization of very practical goals of serious and at times even desperate people.

Becoming a Zen practitioner seems not so much a total and drastic conversion, as is often reported in studies of other groups, but rather a practical and gradual learning process in which the individual experiments and tests the reality of reputed claims to truth. One does not choose something new (as for example one chooses Christ in Pentecostal forms) and reject one's past, as is typical in conversion experiences (Gerlach & Hine, 1970). In fact, the word conversion was used by only one of all the persons interviewed. Instead, the experience that develops in sitting comes to be interpreted by the individual both in terms of Zen and in terms of previous perspectives. The Zen recommendation is "just observe your experience." But one is often disappointed in this effort and needs encouragement to do this difficult work. Both the desirable consequences of relaxation and improved concentration and the so-called worthless experience of *makyo* (hallucinations, etc.) are often taken as desirable, if not always pleasurable, aspects of "being high." They are spoken of, traded, and enjoyed with others as landmarks on one's path. These experiences are taken as indicators of successful sitting and spiritual development.[4] In trying to share with nonsitters the meaning and the impact of sitting, one finds the need to compare meditation with drug or therapeutic experiences, for example. This legitimates a sitter's new activity in the eyes of significant others (Gordon, 1974). Therapeutic vocabularies of motive occurred particularly in response to the question, "Why do you continue to sit?" Common responses are "to get away from craziness," and "to improve the quality of my life." The fact that sitting usually improves health can hardly be overlooked. These interpretations are regularly given to self and others by way of encouraging continued sitting and demonstrating supposed progress.

As one continues to sit, as one gains more experience observing and thus slowing the internal dialogue, the more flashy effects of sitting reportedly diminish. Some people report being discouraged by the lack of these unofficially defined indicators of successful sitting or of other anticipated results. Some actually stop sitting or are discouraged, just as Becker found happening to marijuana users who lost the ability to detect the effects of smoking.

Despite some discouragement by the diminution of spectacular effects, however, the ability to concentrate tends to improve with practice to the point where one is able to experience feelings and insights and to recognize these as the more substantial consequences of sitting. Just as in Becker's example of the musician who "jammed" on the same tune for two hours and recognized this as a consequence of having smoked, Zen students who persist gradually come to recognize an increased ability to give themselves to the situation as a consequence of sitting. Because any self-consciousness interferes with concentration, students are encouraged to give up all expectations. More senior practitioners report that early expectations evaporated and were replaced with a sense of a clear, open present moment. Tipton (1979) quotes practitioners who recognize meditation as giving rise to appropriate action in any situation. They point to an increased ability to interact more spontaneously with others or to maintain a constant state of mind without succumbing to endless and often rigid interpretations. This clarity or constancy – what could perhaps be called "interactional competence" or "the judicial attitude" (Mead, 1934, 169) – comes to be recognized by the student as a result of sitting because it is commonly experienced to increase during and after periods of intense sitting and decrease after periods of no sitting. This response, by the way, is just the opposite of what some marijuana users find when they increase their consumption of the drug. As marijuana use increases there is typically a decreased ability, or motivation, to cope with details and an increased irritability with the world as it presents itself.

This chapter has examined the process of learning to do sitting meditation and the consequences of sitting. Learning to become a Zen practitioner is strikingly similar to learning to use marijuana for pleasure, because both are based in physiological bodymind states that are cultivated by a certain technique and that require interaction with others to identify and learn the meaning of the consequences. Further, it is an experimental process of studying the self, similar in some interesting ways to that proposed by phenomenology. While Zen meditation often occurs in a group setting, the work is inwardly focused by each individual. The nature and type of social relationships and social pressure is considerably different from those considered in the main models of conversion and commitment. While it is suggested by some that new religious groups drastically resocialize and even brainwash members into new attitudes and behaviors, the above analysis suggests that considerably more is involved in the process. Certainly new meanings are learned, but the learning that occurs in examining oneself and taken-for-granted reality in meditative practice is not equivalent to simply replacing, forcefully or otherwise, one group's reality with another's. This point is pursued throughout the remaining pages of this study.

CHAPTER VI

Meditation as a Social Phenomenon: II

In Chapter V, I provided an analysis and some descriptive details of what goes on in the Zen setting, especially what beginners tend to experience and how they go about making collective sense of their experience. This chapter briefly examines another view of how social actors make collective sense of their experience – namely, the social construction of reality school of thought. In the process of examining some of the assumptions and concepts used by this school, we will find that, as usually conceived, it has shortcomings that make this view less than adequate for understanding settings in which meditative practices are used. The remainder of the chapter develops a scheme for viewing meditation as a social phenomenon and for adapting the constructionist view to the study of groups using meditative practices.

The Social Constructionist View

This theoretical posture is roughly phenomenological in assumptions and interests, although it also includes some varieties of symbolic interactionism (Straus, 1981). It is concerned with showing how members of a group go about constructing a world of common experience. It is worthwhile to outline briefly the main points of this posture because the logic of subsequent chapters takes it for granted.

The style of Husserlian phenomenology that has been most influential among sociologists, the "lifeworld" *(Lebenswelt)* approach (Wagner, 1973), emphasizes the importance of language for understanding how social actors come to produce, agree on, and sanction a particular form of social reality. Along with others, they argue that humans normally are in a state, sometimes called the "natural stance," wherein they are unaware of the work they do individually and collectively, to maintain a sense of a world that can be taken for granted. We normally experience the world

65

as if it were an object existing prior to our perception of it. This error, this naive realism, must be exposed if we are to progress to a more adequate understanding of the social world. If the world is not given, independent of our experience, how is it constituted? What kinds of work must social actors do just to come to experience a sense of taken-for-grantedness?

The lifeworld perspective takes the form-giving elements in language as the basic building blocks of social reality. Any particular language contains various kinds of "things" that are supposedly found in the world. There are kinds of people, kinds of situations in which these people are involved, kinds of problems, and kinds of solutions to these problems – all contained within the language a group of people share. People use these typifications to decide what is going on in a particular situation – that is, in a particular present. Any particular language, however, tends to be socially distributed, which is to say that what an individual or a group is familiar with in terms of language (kinds of things and their interrelationships) depends on their particular location in a set of social relationships. There is a social distribution of knowledge that corresponds to what structuralists identify as the social distribution of scarce resources in a society – that is, the regularities of differences in class, status, and political power. These differences, both within a particular society and among various societies, give rise to more or less coherent meaning production systems called "lifeworlds," or various loci of "local" knowledges. Each, according to this perspective, has equal claim to truth, and thus are equally relative ways of knowing (Schutz, 1967).

From this viewpoint, what occurs in meditative practices and the settings that use them is merely the learning of alternative typification schemes that, because they are rooted in Asian cultural forms, are thought to be more collectivistic. It appears that one is being resocialized into the cultural modality of a preindustrial social context and sensitivity (Wagner, 1973; Wolff, 1976). This approach is not entirely wrong but is clearly inadequate.[1] Part of the problem arises from the fact that studies of conversion rarely deal with what goes on in settings that have meditative practices.[2] Instead, the lifeworld perspective popularized by Berger and Luckmann (1966) is used to make theoretical sense of these phenomena. Both authors are students of religion, so their view of religious reality construction is particularly relevant for our purposes. Their discussion of conversion is indicative of the common assumptions of this approach, as well as its shortcomings, and can be used as a tool for seeing both the Zen and meditative settings in general.

Writing of religious conversion, Berger and Luckmann note:

To have a conversion experience is nothing much. The real thing is to be able to keep on taking it seriously: to retain a sense of its plausibility. *This* is where the religious community comes in. It provides the indispensable plausibility structure for the new reality. (1966, 145)

[Conversion] thus involves a reorganization of the conversational apparatus. The partners in significant conversation change. And in conversation with the new significant others subjective reality is transformed. It is maintained by continuing conversation with them, and within the community they represent. Put simply, this means that one must now be very careful with whom one talks. (1966, 146)

Two points stand out about this treatment of religious conversion. First, Berger and Luckmann treat "conversion experience" very lightly (by saying it "is nothing much") and in so doing indicate a lack of interest in how such experience is produced. My central concern, on the contrary, is with understanding the social organization of the "conversion" experience, and I do not assume, at least in the setting of the present study, that the experience comes easily. Second, the emphasis on selective talk as the mechanism for organizing an experience of reality and of maintaining its meaning is to be expected, given the lifeworld perspective. This position is certainly important and useful and is taken especially seriously by some sociologists (cf. Wieder, 1974, as an example of the ethnomethodological approach). My objection is not that talk with others who share the same language and meanings is not important, but rather that this sort of analysis is particularly limited for grasping some essential mechanisms for reality production in meditative settings. Conversation is undeniably central if particular beliefs and propositions about the nature of reality are to be maintained because each reality is merely a "local" construction that has its basis in the shared linguistic categories and practices of a particular social setting. Talk is the way of interpreting collectively the meaning of "events." In certain kinds of settings, however, talk is deemphasized. Whenever experience rather than beliefs or propositional knowledge about reality is valued, arrangements for maintaining silence are often made. To begin to talk with others or with oneself (to think, in Mead's terms) is to move into another modality separate from this experience entirely.

Sudnow (1979) states this point well. He tells of listening to a rock-and-roll band and being immediately impressed by their lack of skill. His thoughts ran to how and why they were so. But when his thinking stopped, the experience of the music changed, and he says he became appreciatively involved with the music and its beauty.

It might be said that I brought more to the music than what existed in it, that its beauty was being sympathetically created rather than discovered by my engrossment, that it has its beauty or not quite apart from my state of mind, that the musicians themselves would say their sounds were amateurish and rough, and even, perhaps, that that was their intention. But any argument that comes to the defense of a distinction in such terms shares in common with any other argument – no matter how sophisticated or commonsensical, no matter what side is taken, no matter what the grounds – the liability that such an evaluation is itself allowed to be relevant. As such, *it would stand outside what is an authentic experience of thoughtless listening.* (1979, 85–6; emphasis added)

Zen Buddhism shares with Taoism ("those who say do not know; those who know do not say") an explicit rejection of the value of talk as a mechanism for contacting and communicating essential knowledge. In fact, interviews with practitioners have shown a movement toward an attitude of "I don't know" as one matures in the practice. I received the following answers in response to my question, "Why do you continue to sit?"

(pause) I don't know. It feels right to do it. (no. 25, 4)

I don't know. I just do it. Sometimes I expect it to do something for me. Here you never know when the return for your effort is going to pop up. (no. 21, 4)

This is what I want to do. I don't know why. (no. 2, 4)

I ask myself that everytime I hit the L.A. Freeway [from San Diego]. (no. 17, 4)

I don't know. Maybe I'm afraid to stop. (no. 28, 4)

I don't know.... I know that if I don't do it I don't feel, in a variety of ways, as good as if I do it. That's an interesting thing. It was much easier two or three years ago to say why I was involved in Zen than it is to explain it now. (no. 62, 4)

What appears to beginners in Zen to be a rule against talking too much reflects, perhaps, more the difficulty of talking about meditative experience at all without placing it in commonsense categories. The word "intuition" is sometimes used to refer to the process whereby meditative insights are produced. Whatever this might imply, it is clear that these experiences, states, or insights have a certain independence from verbal reflective processes. Because of this, the social organization of Zen practice needs to be revealed using techniques of description and analysis that of course include talk but are not limited to it. This deemphasis on talk in the Zen setting, when incorporated into members' practices, makes an alternative to the lifeworld approach to the study of meditative settings particularly useful and, indeed, essential.

This observation about the limits of reflexive processes in meditative settings is supported in the work of another student of the new religious forms. Although Wuthnow (1976) does not deal with meditation explicitly, he does note that those groups that use meditative practices, and some others as well, can be seen as sharing a meaning system that emphasizes direct, intense, personal experience. This important feature has an impact on the kind of meaning system Wuthnow finds associated with these groups.

Whereas cognitive modes of consciousness may consist of point-by-point arguments that address specific questions about meaning and purpose, the mystical mode is more likely to consist simply of a vague feeling that life does indeed make sense. (1976, 124)

Wuthnow's point is well taken. There *is* something special about meaning and conversion in meditative settings, and it is this specialness that the present study attempts to identify and relate to social organization.[3]

The need for a reconsideration of approaches to the study of conversion is appreciated from another quarter as well. Heirich (1977) reviews the main ways conversion is used in social-science literature and finds that it usually means a drastic change in belief and behavior, or a less drastic but still qualitative change in experience and commitment. This literature, he argues, usually deals with the causes of conversion and identifies conversion as a fantasy escape from stress, a result of previous socialization, or a result of the influence of those with whom one is most closely involved. Heirich does not favor the theoretical basis of this treatment of conversion, and his analysis of the evidence that supposedly supports such claims also leads him to reject these proposals. His suggestions for how he thinks conversion might be studied more fruitfully are interesting. Previously, conversion studies have asked the question, Who will change and when? Heirich prefers to ask questions that deal with how "root reality" is destroyed and rediscovered.

An attempt to answer these questions would tie the study of conversion more closely to the growing body of literature that treats religion less as "systems of truth" than as efforts to discover a *ground of being* that orients and orders experience more generally. (1977, 674; emphasis added)

Heirich's approach is especially desirable, even necessary, to appreciate what is involved in "conversion" involving meditative practices. Use of this approach means going beyond socialization theory as it is currently used, not only by sociologists concerned with the study of the causes of religious behavior but also by those addressing how people engage in religious conversion. A recent text summarizes the basic assumption of this theory.

Conversion is essentially a form of resocialization similar to nonreligious resocialization. Through interaction with *believers*, the recruit comes to share their worldview and takes on a new self consistent with that meaning system. (McGuire, 1981, 72; emphasis added)

If this statement adequately describes general constructionist approaches to conversion (it seems to, although two exceptions are Lofland & Skonovd, 1981; and Wilson, 1984), then this school of thought is in no position to deal adequately with meditative settings.

Thus, there does seem to be something special about meditative settings, and Zen settings in particular, that makes not only a lifeworld approach but also the social learning approach of symbolic interaction (see Chapter V) less than adequate. In our brief review of selected literature, we have found that the constructionist view puts exclusive emphasis on talk and language as *the* reality production mechanism; neglects the question of how a conversion or religious experience is produced; and treats conversion as mere resocialization. As we will discuss, the constructionist view can be adapted to deal with those settings and practices (e.g., meditative) that produce altered states of consciousness, experiences of Being, or religious experience. The emphasis on direct experience rather than on talk, belief, or propositional knowledge makes an alternative approach desirable.

Meditation Defined

Meditation is the basic activity that, from the viewpoint of the present study, constitutes Zen practice as a special social phenomenon. Without accomplishment in meditation, the practitioner of Zen is merely a member of a curious imported religious form. Meditation is the key mechanism for understanding how one becomes a member of a Zen group and for appreciating the sorts of changes the member goes through in the process of joining and maturing in Zen practice. Of course, other features of the Zen setting also complement the impact of meditation on the practitioner. Collectively these are taken as constituting a holistic practice – that is, one in which the separation of body and mind is not justified.

Unfortunately, meditation as a word tends to freeze into objectified forms a set of attitudes and practices that have been used by humans intuitively, more or less consciously, throughout the history of the species. To think of meditation then as contained in specific forms such as Yoga, Sufi dancing, Christian contemplation, or Zen sitting is to miss its unobtrusive presence in everyday life and consciousness.[4]

For purposes of the present study, meditation refers to "a family of techniques which have in common a conscious attempt to focus attention in a non-analytical way, and an attempt not to dwell on discursive, ruminating thought" (Shapiro, 1980, 14).[5] As Wilber (1980, 1981, 1983) points out, meditation has nothing to do with the occult or with psychotic experiences, as is sometimes supposed by those with opinions on this topic. Instead, Eliade argues to work on one's consciousness is not to isolate oneself from the real, nor to lose oneself in dreams or hallucinations; on the contrary, it is to make direct contact with life, to force one's way into the concrete. To meditate is to rise to planes of reality inaccessible to the profane. (1969, 198)

More specifically, meditation is often said to have two important consequences that are directly relevant to the concerns of social science. First, it leads to a deconditioning of the practitioner (Eliade, 1969, xvi–xvii; Wilber, 1980, 93–9). Second, it increases the ability to concentrate or to observe the mind in operation (Brown, 1977; Kapleau, 1967; Tart, 1975). Both of these claims need to be examined more closely because they are central to the view of Zen practice found in this book.

Deconditioning

Conditioning and deconditioning are terms that are usually associated with behaviorist learning theory, which is, in its psychological forms at least, characterized by two views. First, unlike the constructionist perspective, no use is made of consciousness or of subjective, self-reflexive states. Emphasis is put instead on measurable relationships between the organism and the conditioning environment. Second, behaviorism looks

Indicators of the Japanese aesthetic that tends to prevail at the Los Angeles Center.

for and finds influences on an individual's behavior that tend to produce similar behavior in all situations. The way the term "deconditioning" is used in this study draws attention to effects of meditation as an alteration in body and mind state and reality-construction practices that are not usually admitted by, or considered relevant to, socialization theory.

Social theory necessarily must assume some sort of "normal" consciousness, an orientation to or motivation typical of everyday life (e.g., the calculating mentality of the actor in exchange theory, the natural attitude in Schutz, and "life is basically a struggle for status" in Collins). An inadvertent consequence of these assumptions has been that all people are assumed to be in the same modality, only more or less advantaged in their location in the distribution of the scarce resources of wealth, status, and power. In this view, those persons doing meditative religious practices, for example, are reaping status rewards vis-à-vis other religious forms and groups. They are sometimes labeled "esoteric" by social scientists, meaning they practice "a private ritual, often accompanied by a secret mythology and language" (Johnson, 1982, 33). No effort is spent, however, to deal with these forms as special or different from the ordinary in any significant way because the initial assumption of there being a "normal" mentality precludes it.

Deconditioning as I use the term seeks to break with this common assumption typical of socialization theory of a normal consciousness that is common to all and within which all conversion experiences occur or, at best as in the case of Berger and Luckmann (1966), their plausibility is maintained. It draws attention to forms of bodymind training in meditative practices, and Zen practice in particular, that tend to cultivate a way of being, a set of dispositions (ways of thinking, feeling, acting) that Wilber (1981) has called the "causal" level of religious sensitivity and cognitive structuralization.[6]

In contrast to the behaviorist view of conditioning, which completely ignores subjective, reflexive processes and situational contingencies, this study (following the writings of classical and contemporary students of meditation) values both (albeit within limits) and keeps them in the analysis. I argue that sustained and informed meditation and Zen practices in general produce a cognitive and emotional stability that allows more balanced and judicious judgment and more effective action in particular situations. A student of consciousness, who argues in favor of just such a claim, offers a clear statement of some of the problems with everyday awareness.

In the ordinary ... [consciousness, mind] is often hyperactive to the point of constituting noise.... You cannot hear your senses over the noise of your thoughts.... Something happens, you think about it, reach a decision, and act, which changes the situation and makes you reevaluate it. Or you do not act, but thinking about it reminds you of something else, which reminds you of something else, about which you make a decision, which results in action that modifies another situation, which starts more evaluation and association processes. For example, someone on the street asks me for money, which starts me thinking about disinterested charity versus the work ethic ... and I'm so involved in this thought process that I do not notice various perceptual cues that would inform me about this person's situation and intentions. (Tart, 1975, 116)

Seen in this way, then, meditation is a process of learning (or, better, unlearning) that can be said to involve deconditioning of both personal and socially shared habits and processes of reality construction. The process of becoming a member of a group with meditative practices is not just the learning of a new symbolic universe and role (as socialization theory suggests), but a transformation of one's body and mind in the disciplined examination of the origins of one's thoughts, their close articulation with body states (feeling, emotions), and their replacement by still more thoughts and feelings. This process is closely tied to the second important consequence of meditative practice – an increase in the ability to concentrate.

Concentration

In a pioneering but neglected work, Kurt Wolff (1976) undertakes the study of the circumstances of concentration because, he argues, concentration is closely related to "surrender" or the "experience of being." Being is a mode of existence in which the "the everyday subject disappears in the identification with its object" (p. 165). He finds this happening in intellectual work, art, and religion. "When I am writing, I am that which is writing; still more accurately: I have disappeared and all there is is 'there's writing' or 'there's writing going on' or 'writing' " (p. 177). The relevance of this experience for doing sociology is what his book is about. He notes, however, that despite the importance and value of this experience of being, it happens very infrequently. Instead one usually does not disappear at all but self-consciously strives to impose one's will on the world (e.g., the writing process).

Despite the value of his work as a pathbreaking effort in addressing this topic sociologically, Wolff has little to say about the various forms of concentration.[7] He recognizes its importance but his discussion remains at a basic level perhaps because it is tied to the phenomenological practice of "bracketing."

Bracketing and Meditation

The practice called bracketing, reduction, or epoché is associated with some phenomenological views of reality construction. From the phenomenological viewpoint, the "natural attitude" of everyday life takes the world for granted and thus remains naive of its social construction in the processes and practices of language use and interaction with others. Sociology done in this attitude also remains less than essential and often resembles a sort of "folk sociology" (Wieder, 1974), because it uses the language and explanations of members and leaves unexamined the basic building blocks of the social world and shared reality. Doing a "reduction" supposedly allows one to return to that which is primitive in experience, namely one's consciousness of the world as it is coming into being for an individual moment after moment. It attempts to see through the familiar world of everyday life into the elements that compose it. This approach involves putting one's belief in the existence of the world and even oneself in brackets – that is, not denying them, but supposing they do not exist. Nothing is left but the consciousness of things, conceptions, judgments, feelings, and so forth. One may indeed still perceive a chair, but it is the chair as one perceives it, not as it exists. It is the phenomenon "chair" as it appears to one individual. What remains as real is the consciousness of the thought "chair as it appears to me" (paraphrased from Schutz, 1967, 106). Merleau-Ponty provides a different perspective.

Reflection [bracketing] does not withdraw from the world toward the unity of consciousness as the world's basis; it steps back to watch the forms of transcendence fly up like sparks from a fire; it slackens the intentional threads which attach us to the world and thus brings them to our notice; it alone is conscious of the world because it reveals that world as strange and paradoxical. (1962, xiii)

This method is promising but, as Wagner (1973) has noted, many sociologists (among others) have had difficulty using it. Because it is associated with the early work of Husserl, which assumes the possibility of a Pure Ego and involves essential perceptions, this method is usually considered to have solipsistic difficulties. Too much emphasis is put, it is argued, on the experience of the individual and not enough on how this experience comes to be shared with others. More narrowly, its problem is that it contradicts the sociology of knowledge that finds knowledge tied to an individual's and group's social location, a tie that is not simply removed by some "psychological" or (it is supposed) narrowly cognitive technique such as bracketing.[8]

Regardless of one's view of the relative merits of bracketing, the hard reality remains that it is extremely difficult to break with habitual ways of thinking and organizing (intending) experience that have been done day in and day out all of one's life. Doing a phenomenological reduction successfully is an accomplishment that takes discipline and practice.

This difficulty is confirmed by Sekida (1975, 191), who suggests that the practice of bracketing is quite similar to Zen meditation. Both practices are efforts to stop (however briefly in the case of bracketing) the routine activity of consciousness and in the process to gain more adequate knowledge of oneself and reality. What we have noted on the basis of the experience of those who have developed skill in doing meditative practices, however, is that it often takes years of serious practice to sustain a distance from the habits of routine consciousness. It cannot be done by mere wishing nor can it be understood as a process that is limited to intellectual activities alone (although many commonly assume this). When it is done, however, the increased ability to concentrate or to observe the mind in operation provides the basis of insight into, and awareness of, reality-construction processes quite unlike those of either science or common sense. This claim is supported by recent research on meditation by Western scholars.

Some Consequences of Meditative Practice

Scientific studies done in the last few decades have identified some common consequences of meditation.[9] The main physiological consequences are:

1. reduced skin conductance (galvanic skin response) that is often taken as an indication of reduced cognitive anxiety (Schwartz, Davidson, & Goleman, 1980);
2. increases in alpha rhythms, as shown on an electroencephalogram, which are often associated with feelings of well-being (Banquet, 1973; Hirai, 1974); and
3. decreases in oxygen consumption, respiratory rate, heart rate, and blood pressure, all of which are often taken as indicators of reduced somatic anxiety (Frumkin, Nathan, Prout, & Cohen, 1978; Wallace, Benson, & Wilson, 1971).

In summary, there seems to be a reduction of stress and increased relaxation that manifest both cognitively and somatically. The exact impact of such indicators on feeling, thought, and action is far from definite, of course, and even these indicators tend to vary considerably over the career of any particular meditator (Brown, 1977), making their meaning difficult to specify without reference to more subjective reports of experience in meditation. In general, however, and in light of these qualifications, I believe that the minimal consequences of meditative practices are a reduction of anxiety, a slowing of the internal dialogue, and a diminishing of excessive emotional energy. This alteration of dispositions has immediate consequences for feeling, thought, and action.

Other investigators with scientific interests, but who rely on the reports of subjective experience by practitioners of some form of meditation, have made some relevant observations. Even those who are not well skilled in doing meditation often have intense experiences such as hallucinations, sadness, and a feeling of merging with objects. Further, the content of meditative experience, in the opinion of these researchers, cannot be reduced to the belief systems of the meditators – that is, their experience is not merely a reproduction of what they expect to find. At a certain level of meditative experience, persons of diverse cultural backgrounds tend to encounter "a) feeling of incommunicability, b) transcendence of sense modalities, c) absence of specific content, such as images and ideas, and d) feelings of unity with the ultimate" (Shapiro, 1980, 205). These findings are supported by the classic texts of those religious traditions with meditative practices. What these texts have in common is the claim that a hierarchy of altered states of awareness is available as one becomes more adept at doing meditation (e.g., Brown, 1977). This similarity of meditative experience across various traditions is summarized by Maliszewski, Twemlow, Brown, and Engler (1981).

Upon close inspection of the classic texts, the sequence of experiences reported within the concentration meditation traditions and the changes reported within the mindfulness approaches did *not* vary greatly from one meditation system to the next. Although there were noticeable differences in the progression of meditation experiences, the phenomenological reports themselves exhibited a highly similar underlying psychological organization when analyzed longitudinally (i.e., along the progression of experiences taking place from the beginning through the end of a meditative path). On the other hand, differences in the phenomenological features *were* found in terms of how most of the meditative systems conceptualized and described those states of consciousness associated with the culmination of a particular path. (1981, 10)

Finally, these studies found that those persons usually available for study in the United States and other Western countries are beginners in terms of their level of accomplishment in doing meditative practice. The implication of this last point is that when practitioners become more thoroughly accomplished, the impact will be even greater.[10]

This information is fascinating and immediately challenges the sociologist to deal with it in understanding the process called conversion. It allows not only a glimpse of the possibilities of developing concentration skills by means of practices institutionalized in groups with viable meditative traditions, but also raises the question of how the processes of such traditions produce essentially similar experiences among their practitioners. Because these go well beyond what individuals have been able to accomplish by themselves without institutionalized support, one can expect to find a quality of experience significantly different from that common to settings without such meditative practices. Groups with such practices ought to prove interesting to sociologists and others concerned with the process of how some groups arrive at an experience of "root reality" and how they come to agree on the meaning of this experience.

The increased levels of concentration and related altered states of consciousness that are developed in meditative practices are directly relevant for understanding religious experience and the processes of conversion and commitment in meditative settings. As will be seen in Chapters VII, VIII, and IX, these heightened states of concentration are central to the ways of organizing reality in Zen and other meditative settings. They are directly experienced by members who are able to do meditation adequately and intensively enough to raise this bodymind condition. They make a certain sense of commonality and understanding possible among members by providing common experiences and cognitive categories that limit the need for recourse to discursive speech. Furthermore, these states of concentration are common to all meditative traditions and practices to a degree, although some Christians argue a basic difference in form and content of religious experience (e.g., Dumoulin, 1963; Johnston, 1978), and allow a common understanding across group lines among those groups that encounter such states. However, it may also lead to misunderstanding among those groups not encountering such states of concentration who often insist that all forms of religious practice and doctrine be judged in terms of their propositional consistency or scriptural purity.

These findings lend support to the claim that meditative practices are effective for producing alterations in usual ways of perceiving, feeling, and acting in everyday life. They stop far short of the kind of detailed information necessary, however, to understand this sort of activity as reality-building practices. To achieve this understanding involves turning from studies that are limited to purely scientific interests to those that more clearly describe meditative experience with an interest in understanding how it is produced and its meaning agreed on in a socially organized setting.

CHAPTER VII

Doing Zen Meditation

The emphasis on the importance of the body in meditative practices developed in Chapter VI is supported by a contemporary sociologist who also recognizes the key role of practice in knowing and doing. This chapter briefly reviews Sudnow's *Ways of the Hand*, which can serve as an exemplar for examining Zen meditation.

Sudnow's View of Improvised Conduct

In his preface to *Ways of the Hand*, Sudnow insists that his is a descriptive effort, phenomenologically inspired, done from the viewpoint of the actor, using a fine examination of concrete problems posed by the task of sustaining an orderly activity, focused on the body's improvisational ways, and not using introspective consciousness (1978, xiii). He might be seen as trying to make the phenomenological bracketing process empirically available in the details of jazz improvisation. I want to use his work as an exemplar, but I also want to do some explanation, some analysis, not just description. What is especially valuable in Sudnow's work is his emphasis on the body doing improvisation. By attending to how the body looks and works rather than to the ideas, rules, tactics recommended, theories of music, scales, and so on, he comes to know about the body and how jazz improvisation is done by that body. In the process of coming to focus on how the hands go about learning to do improvisation, he comes to experience a change in consciousness that he notes at the end of the book. This change in consciousness, which results indirectly from a sustained, disciplined practice, is also directly relevant to our interests and purposes.

Sudnow outlines the process of the training of the hands and the increasing subtlety of their skill. In the earliest stages of learning he reports:

My beginning piano lessons entailed the acquisition of working ability with a host of concepts about the keyboard. In order to play jazz I had to learn about what a "song" was, what "chords" were, and how chords could be located and produced on the keyboard. (1978, 2)

The emphasis at this beginning stage, he notes, was on rules, scales, and ideas about jazz because the hands were relatively untrained in moving on the keyboard and in making jazz sounds. With practice he came to be able to make jazz sounds but still felt his progress was insufficient.

I was listening-in-order-to-make-my-way. . . . But it is one thing to recognize familiar sounds you are making and another to be able to aim for particular sounds to happen. A different sort of directionality of purpose and potential for action is involved in each case. (1978, 38)

A second plateau in his music came with what he calls the ability to "go for the sounds." He notes that this going for the sounds, this melodic intentionality, only emerged slowly, as he acquired the necessary skills. He was not trying to do it earlier and failing. Rather as the hands became more and more familiar with the keyboard and pathways around it, this form of intending melodies became possible. At this stage the hands and their skillful movements through the terrain of the keyboard already replaced ideas, rules about chords, and scales as "source" of the music.

A third very different way of playing emerged with practice for Sudnow, one that he calls "going for the jazz." In this later stage, the earlier effort of reaching for a particular sound or series of notes is, when jazz really happens, replaced by jazz being done without being intended except in a general sense.

I began to join up in a new partnership with the hands and the sounding terrain, as where we were going together began to slowly integrate into an altogether new way of doing singing at the piano: a new way for intentions to be formed, a new sort of synchrony and directionality of linkage between my head's aiming for sung sounds and my fingers' aiming for singable sounds, becoming progressively shaped and refined. (1978, 95–6)

Springboard – get the beat right – keep the hands loose and flexible – bounce around on a place – go for a long reach – breathe deeply – do interweavings – relax – don't go fast until you're ready. (1978, 146–7)

These quotes illustrate the gradual transformation of his way of doing music and of intending melodies. Intentionality changes in form as the hands become more trained and more skilled at doing activities at the keyboard. Who it is that initiates a melody seems to change in the direction away from "the speaking I." What the player knows, according to Sudnow, is increasingly tied to what the hands can do over a particular course and in a particular place. Intentionality moves ever closer to the hands, or becomes a more integrated bodily activity closely tied to, and limited by, the hands' capabilities or "ways." This eventually brings him to raise the question of who is in fact making the music. He concludes:

I sing with my fingers, so to speak, and only so to speak, for there is a new "I" that the speaking I gestures toward with a pointing at the music that says: It is a singing body and this I (here, too, so to speak) sings. (1978, 152)

Using Sudnow to See Zen Practice Sociologically

What is of particular interest in Sudnow's work?

1. The sense of self changes (or can be perceived to change)
2. in the course of a sustained, diligent practice; and
3. the role of the body is seen as central
4. in the production of spontaneous, improvised yet normatively organized conduct.

The first of these points concerning the self is interesting because it is linked with the notion of intentionality. Intentionality is, roughly, the tenet of phenomenology that consciousness is always consciousness of some "thing." Consciousness is always directed to some object whose form and meaning are constituted by the interests, cognitive presuppositions, and practices of those persons in question. One of these objects is the individual self. To speak, as Sudnow does, of a change in intentionality means that he experiences a difference in how "he" participates in the playing of jazz or how jazz gets done.

Beginning to learn to play jazz, he experiences himself, as is supposedly the case in everyday life, as in control, in charge of making the movements on the keys with his fingers so that they sound the way jazz is supposed to sound. In the beginning this takes the form of learning jazz scales and tunes – that is, following the rules. He moves away from this posture somewhat in the second stage of playing, but even at this stage he is still trying to make it happen. The third stage of "going for the jazz," where jazz improvisation actually begins to occur, is recognized almost imperceptively, as if it is, to a degree, independent of his willing, knowing, and doing. Certainly he intends to play, but how it gets done in its particulars is in his experience, not of his doing. This account of how this change in awareness is related to practice provides us with a way of looking at Zen practice and its consequences sociologically.

The second point, the importance of practice, is of particular interest because it tends to contradict how sociologists often try to account for conduct. As noted in Chapter IV, most theories see social action determined by values and norms on the one hand or by clearly defined verbal ideas (definition of the situation, role taking) on the other (cf. Collins, 1981).

Third, Sudnow argues for the importance of the body in the production of social phenomena and illustrates empirically a case of how it happens. In illustrating the structuring of intentionality and its rootedness in bodily movement, he writes:

A way of listening is a way of using the body to take hold of a course of movements, which makes listening a course of activity itself. While we can reduce the movement to objects and construct a theory of communication, what we need for an approach to intersubjectivity is an embodied description of the course of gestures instead of a cognitive attack on the problem of minds. (1979, 83)

This concern with embodiment is unusual in social studies. In fact such studies

have assumed that since the body is composed of universal features, it necessarily is experienced as such; furthermore, given this "universality," it need not be accounted for within any special system of propositions bearing on the explanation of human behavior. (Manning & Fabrega, 1973, 254)

In disagreeing with this common assumption, Manning and Fabrega develop some propositions about self and body. The following are especially relevant for my purposes.

The *body* and *self* are not seen as logically distinguishable entities: they form a continuum. Changes in one produces and cannot be separated from changes in the other. (1973, 287)

The body is seen as a wholistic, integrated aspect of the self and social relations which is vulnerable and may be easily affected by feelings, other people, natural forces, or spirits. (1973, 287)

This issue of the importance of the body is addressed by a variety of writers including Bourdieu (1977), Merleau-Ponty (1962, 1968), Natanson (1970), Tambiah (1985), Wilber (1983), Wolff (1976), and Zaner (1964, 1981).[1] Their discussions expand upon nearly all of the topics in this section but also consider topics beyond this study's focus on the process of Zen practice and its consequences. They are cited to lend support for locating the phenomenon of "Zen" in the socially organized processes of body (and mind) training. From now on the expression bodymind is used without further explanation, although the discussion in Chapter VIII will help clarify what I mean by this term.

The fourth point I emphasize in Sudnow's work is the relationship between spontaneity or improvisation and social (normative) organization. What is "normative organization"?[2] For Sudnow it seems to mean that the activity (more accurately, the "conduct") can be recognized clearly as such, especially by those who can accomplish it, and that failures can also be identified. Describing such conduct is not easy, however, as Sudnow notes when he remembers his teacher being curiously vague in his efforts to tell him what he was doing wrong and how he could improve. One does not play jazz according to rules; rather the ability to accomplish jazz improvisation is to be understood as a consequence of skills developed by the hands, or ways of the hands. Rules have their place in pointing to what is or is not the phenomenon, but knowing the rules does not allow one to play appropriately. Embodied skills, gained through long and diligent practice, actually accomplish the task.

Thus, a sociology that attempts to explain or understand a phenomenon such as Zen practice, and members' shared experience therein, by means of rational and cognitive capabilities of social actors alone is doomed to miss the locus of the phenomenon as it is produced. Just as Sudnow finds in the case of jazz improvisation, Zen practice, when it is well done, resists completely the effort to treat it as a reality constituted by rules employed by actors using rational and cognitive practices. But rather than saying that "irrational" practices are at the core of Zen practice, the task is to raise the issue of what is "rational" and to pursue the answer of the question into a description and analysis of Zen practice. The point to be made is not only that Zen practice cannot be adequately accounted for by means of social learning or an unmodified constructionist viewpoint, for example, but that everyday life is such that the issues that are raised in an analysis of Zen practice or jazz improvisation are directly relevant to it as well.

On this basis I will argue in Chapters VIII and IX that Zen practice (and meditative practices in general) is a process of training that cultivates an alternative way of experiencing the body and of consciousness in general. In place of the usual way of seeing the contents of consciousness and their meaning as being formed by language categories and interests, Zen practice is seen as a process of altering and ultimately reducing the influence of language and interests in shaping consciousness. It is a process of reducing intentionality, a way of being more aware and of entering, at least potentially, the realm of human experience at the basis of all "local" knowledges. The importance of such experience for Zen practitioners is its existential, transformative implications. For Merleau-Ponty, however, it is more ontological.

The relationship of subject and object is no longer that cognitive relationship in which the object always appears as constituted by the subject, but it is a relationship of being, through which, to use a paradox, the subject *is* his body, his world, his situation, and in a certain sense enters into interaction with it. (Merleau-Ponty, 1964, 72, quoted in Fontana & van de Water, 1977, 125)

Intentionality, then, can be seen as a variable dimension of our life activity and consciousness. Presuppositions, common linguistic categories, and interactional practices can be seen as highly salient or minimally so. One might envision a continuum ranging from highly reified consciousness and reflexive thinking on the one end where rules, roles, norms, ideas, and interests of various sorts fill the consciousness of the actors, to the other end of the continuum where consciousness is actively engaged in witnessing thought and activity as it emerges. In between are recognizable combinations of these two extremes.

To the extent that Sudnow's exemplar fits, the remainder of this chapter describes in a similar fashion the processes and problems involved in learning to do Zen meditation. In this approach, the description will stay close to the individual's experience of this practice because this is the only way that it can be adequately described and understood. In this description of how one comes to do the practice, changes are seen occurring that are sociologically interesting and that bear on the understanding of how one comes to be able to experience this particular group reality.

By focusing on the naive beginner who has no previous training in meditation, I will show how one gradually begins to experience the impact of Zen practice. As Sudnow recommends, attention will be put specifically on the body. Not that mind and body can be simply separated, but previous sociological studies have usually avoided addressing the body and have emphasized cognition exclusively. It is useful to avoid this one-sidedness so as to appreciate this setting the way an insider comes to experience it. To do this, *zazen* is treated as a practice very roughly analogous to Sudnow's piano practice.

Meditation is often said to have two important consequences that are directly relevant to the concerns of social science: It increases the ability to concentrate, and it leads to a deconditioning of the practitioner. How does the social organization of Zen practice contribute to the production of these consequences?

The Social Organization of Zen Meditation

In beginning to play piano and learn jazz improvisation, Sudnow notes that music theory in the form of songs, chords, scales, and so forth provided the means for proceeding. In a Zen setting, a set of similar basic rules fairly common to all Zen groups can be identified. These rules are referred to hereafter as elements of the social organization of Zen practice and are treated roughly the way Sudnow treats the rules of music theory in his work. They provide the basis for beginning to practice each skill, but they in no way account for how the phenomenon of jazz improvisation or Zen action is actually accomplished by the practitioner.

What the beginner learns in introductory workshops has already been discussed in Chapter IV. The clearest requirements that the beginner feels are behavioral. What am I expected to do so as not to stand out or give offense? When I am with those people, what do I have to do to be comfortable? What are the expectations? One can point to various requirements by noting different ritual occasions in the meditation hall. Besides the requirements of doing sitting meditation *(zazen)*, there are those of walking meditation *(kinhin)*, service (bowing, chanting), and other similar rituals, each having its own tightly prescribed form. These are not so rigidly prescribed that the beginner cannot participate, but rigid enough so that close conformity is expected of more senior students. Let us examine the behavioral requirements and other prescriptions for doing the central activity of Zen practice and the main topic of this chapter, sitting meditation.

Zen meditation exists in a context that is provided by the elements of the social organization of Zen practice. The first of these concerns prescribed meditative *postures*. The beginner is instructed to sit in a position that allows an erect spine and stability over the period of half an hour or so. There are several postures that an individual can legitimately assume – the so-called Burmese position, the half lotus, the *seiza* position, and the full lotus (for illustrations, see Sekida, 1975) – and the beginner attempts to be comfortable in one of them. Usually it is suggested that a position be practiced until it is possible for the beginner to sit still for half an hour. This practice requires some time for most people as the muscles stretch. In Zen meditation the meditator sits on a small round cushion *(zafu)* so that the buttocks are raised higher than the knees and so that the lower abdomen can be pushed slightly forward. The beginner is told to keep the spine erect and the eyes downward at a forty-five degree angle, look at a spot on the floor about three feet in front, hold the hands in a *mudra* or standard position in front of the lower abdomen, and so on. Instructions for sitting postures are explicit, regularly repeated, and continually emphasized as central to the meditation process. More than a mere convention, the sitting posture is seen as essential to the doing of meditation. The body immediately takes on a new importance as soon as one begins to do the practice.

A second element of the social organization of Zen practice concerns prescriptions about what to do with one's "mind." Each practitioner is

Sitting meditation in the Los Angeles zendo. Those students who have been formally inducted into Buddhism wear the *rokuzu,* the biblike cloth piece seen here.

assigned a particular *object of meditation* or at least is guided by the teacher in particular ways of examining the flow of one's consciousness. This particular item or style of one's meditation is referred to by members as one's "practice." In many Zen settings, the first form of practice assigned is the counting of the breath, where inhalations and exhalations are counted from one to ten repeatedly. Difficult to do in the beginning, this practice gradually becomes manageable if one continues with determination. As one masters a particular kind of practice, the teacher usually changes it to a more subtle and demanding form.

A third element is the *organization of the meditation hall*. When people sit together, there are explicit rules, modified somewhat in each particular setting, that are traditional or customarily observed. Some of the basic rules had their origins in the centuries following the introduction of Zen into China around the sixth century A.D. Some rules concern how collective sitting meditation will be done. Once the sitting period has begun (periods are marked by the ringing of a bell by a timekeeper), there is to be no moving, itching, wiggling, looking around, or nose blowing. One is expected to be stock, stone still. All assume reasonably similar postures. All face the wall or the center of the room, depending on the situation; all wear similar kinds of dark clothing. At the end of the period a bell is rung and there are explicitly prescribed ways of getting up from the sitting position and of doing walking meditation. Usually the sitting periods are about thirty minutes long with ten minutes of walking meditation and a chance to go to the bathroom if necessary. It is common to have three or four such sitting periods together before breaking. The rules facilitate concentrating on one's practice and discourage anything that interferes with that concentration.

Much more detail could be given about these rules and how they organize the collective meditative setting, but my purpose here is to note that these rules exist, not to describe them at length. Following Sudnow, I am more concerned with the processes and problems of doing the practice rather than particular rules. In these processes, by confronting these problems, the reality of Zen is accomplished.[3]

Problems in Zen Practice

Two common problems in the sitting process are pain, and actively trying to do meditation. The first of these is perhaps obvious because practitioners are sitting for some time in rather demanding and unusual postures, unusual at least for Westerners. The second, however, requires comment.

According to Schutz (1967), the way we tend to act in everyday life is of two sorts: Either we act habitually, traditionally, and without forethought, or we consciously engage the world with a project in mind that we wish to accomplish (either thinking or working). Schutz calls the first of these "conduct," the second "social action." Both are, or can be, socially meaningful forms. Action is conduct devised in advance. How does this classification bear on the problems of sitting meditation?

Neither stance or attitude is appropriate for doing meditation. What characterizes the first way of acting in everyday life is that it is a relatively passive mode (Schutz, 1967, 213). Benoit (1955) notes that in such a passive mode our perceptions are of the world as preexisting objects. Because we are only passively attentive, we do not notice these objects coming into being and passing away. This passivity contributes to a sense that the world of objects exists in the form we perceive it independent of our perception – the so-called "natural attitude," or "objectivist fallacy." The second way of acting in everyday life (also within the natural attitude) is more active. We have goals or projects that we use to plan and "do" our activity. Schutz argues that in the modality he calls "working," where we engage our bodies in pursuit of these goals, we experience our working self as our total self.

Beginners in Zen practice often enter meditation with this active attitude; in interviews with them I have sometimes heard: "I'm really going to do this stuff [Zen]," or "It won't take me long to get enlightened," and so on. However in this wanting and trying to do it, in this willing in the usual sense of the word, there is a problem. Teachers of all traditions of meditation emphasize that a special attitude is involved in doing meditation, specifically a different engagement of self in the willing process. One must assume what I will call, for lack of a better term, an attitude of "active passivity" – that is, a posture of wakeful attentiveness that is at the same time a nondoing.

Wilber's discussion of Benoit (1955) helps clarify this point. In contrast to the level of attention typical of much of our everyday life, an active, yet relaxed, attention (appropriate for meditation) "lies in wait for the advent of my inner movements. It is no longer my emotions [or thoughts] which interest me, but their coming to birth" (Benoit, cited in Wilber, 1977, 312). This mode of active attention directed at the origins of thoughts and emotions can lead to the stopping of the internal dialogue and thought, and to the production of a clarity that far exceeds that of working.

In this condition an utter mental Silence prevails. This is remaining with what is. . . . The condition of "remaining" in this "isness," this Silence, this Stillness, we will call (after Huang Po) "sitting in a Bodhimandala," that is sitting in a place where enlightenment can erupt at any instant. (Wilber, 1977, 314; emphasis dropped)

When this stopping is complete, it leads to an entirely different mode of knowing, which Wilber (1977, 315) refers to as passive awareness: We always already have this awareness but we do not recognize it as such. For our purposes, we need only to recognize the difficulty of trying to do meditative practices with modes of bodymind that are common in everyday life.[4] Another point is relevant here as well.

Schutz argues that we are most wide-awake in the working modality of action, by which he means that in working we are on "a plane of consciousness of highest tension originating in an attitude of full attention to life and its requirements" (1967, 213). Doing sitting meditation (as opposed to Zen practice in general) is indeed a turning away from the pragmatic requirements of everyday life and thus can justifiably be seen by Schutz's scheme as less "wide-awake" than either thinking or working, which are by definition pragmatically oriented. But, and this is a major objection, if one admits, as Schutz does, the importance of attention or concentration in the constitution of reality, then one needs to consider the experience of meditators and those engaged in broader meditative practices regarding this topic.

Studies of meditation commonly report that meditators find ordinary consciousness to be hazy and dreamlike compared to that encountered in, and facilitated by, meditation (Tart, 1975, 23). Further, this increased concentration or ability to attend can be taken into everyday life – that is, into the activities of thinking or working – with the consequence that these activities are experienced as brighter and more awake as a result. Schutz's point that the working modality tends to be more wide-awake is well taken. This wide-awakeness, however, can be even further enhanced by meditative practices. This process can be seen in an examination of Zen meditation that considers how an individual comes to encounter the two problems of pain on the one hand and actively trying to do meditation on the other, and how practitioners tend to develop, and to be shaped by, this practice. The following account is based on both the author's experience in meditation and that of other practitioners.

An Experience of Sitting Meditation

Stage I

In beginning to do Zen meditation,[5] I found myself very preoccupied with the ideas that I had about what Zen was going to give me or do for me, about my goals of meditation. I had come to Zen from experimentation with psychedelic drugs. I had had some very profound experiences that I wished to experience again, and I supposed that Zen practice would enable me to do this. After a casual reading of Zen texts, I had the sense that Zen teachers and philosophers were in touch with a greater sense of meaning in life and a sense of awe without doing drugs. I set out to produce such experiences. I am not sure why but I felt there was something about how Zen was organized that was important for the production of this experience. At the time I had no sense of engaging in religious activities. I felt myself experimenting (in retrospect in a very mechanistic way) with practices that were tied somehow instrumentally to this desired extraordinary experience. Years later this expectation that Zen experience was going to be psychedelic still interfered with my seeing and appreciating the more subtle dimensions of meditation and my life.

In this early stage of the meditative process, my sitting seemed to me to be hindered by the efforts of the thinking, verbal self. I tried to impose on the body the posture and other requirements of not moving. This became a matter of some pride to me. Not to move until the end of the sitting period was a major commitment, and I had a strong need not to fail in this regard. I felt the social pressure to meet these behavioral demands to be very high.[6]

More than just imposing a posture on my body, I did considerable work to achieve what I expected, in my naïveté, enlightenment to be. I did work, in the sense that Hochschild (1979) means it, to make myself feel what I anticipated (or remembered from psychedelic experience) was desirable and appropriate. Needless to say, my efforts failed, although some very curious states were generated.[7]

The body at this stage objected. I had a history of lower-back problems, and sitting was experienced as an interesting feeling because the muscles across the lower back began to stretch, as I (in overdoing, that is misunderstanding, the recommended posture) stretched the spine erect and held it so for half an hour at a time. I noticed a change in the muscles of the lower back and it changed (not to say improved) the way I felt. I began to associate that with success in meditation as any change in the way one experiences the body can be taken as a positive sign in this regard. The body adapted very gradually to the demands of the sitting posture – so gradually in fact that I hardly realized its coming to be more comfortable in doing meditation.

At this beginning stage, I was largely in my "head" or almost entirely in verbal consciousness, almost completely cut off from my body (so it seemed). Only as the body came to "complain" about the posture, did I focus my attention on it. And complain it did. I experienced my body at this point in the practice as something like, "Of course I have a body and it is scientifically absurd to think otherwise." But in this certainty I remained almost entirely limited in my experience to being "up in the head" as a thinking and seemingly controlling entity – that is, an actively willing entity. This awareness of the body was largely theoretical knowledge about it and its functions rather than an intimacy with it. This relationship would change as my ability to do meditation increased.

At this stage, I found it extremely difficult to count the breath from one to ten. Sometimes I would lose count even before getting to two, and other times I found my counting to be at thirteen. My mind was undisciplined. Distractions of thoughts and bodily pain and tensions took me away from the task of counting my breath. Instructions for meditation say just come back to counting when you notice you have lost track. In that coming back time and time again, it is said there is improvement in the ability to attend. In doing this, however, there was often no tangible result. I got sick of doing it, especially doing it poorly. I got sick of the pain in the legs, the endless fantasies, and constant diversions. In trying to pay attention to breathing but failing, I became annoyed with the everyday flow of my undisciplined mind. The more fantasy, the less concentration, the greater the pain became. Despite my explicit commitment to remaining still and maintaining a posture, for whatever reasons, until the bell would mark the end of the sitting period, I even tried moving but gained no relief. Changing my position completely would help but this was out of the question. The pain was there – the pain of the body and the pain of the fantasies. Another unsuccessful tactic was to daydream through the period, but in an extended retreat period *(sesshin)* where the pain is most intense, trying to deny where you are by fantasizing fails completely. It simply makes the reality harder to bear. Efforts to avoid the present by daydreaming actually aggravated the pain.

In the early stage of practice, it is common to have the urge to control the breathing process and impose an order on it by counting. One way this is done is by tensing up around the pain and counting to oneself, oooonnnnnnnneeeee, while forcing the breath out, tttttwwwwwwwooooooooooo, while forcefully contracting the muscles of the lower abdomen, forcing the diaphragm to push the air out. In this way, I tried to impose on the body something that I hoped would provide an escape from the pain and frustration. The theoretical understanding I had of what it meant to count the breath became, at this early stage, the Procrustian bed into which the body and its processes were forced. In retrospect it seems something I could not avoid. D. T. Suzuki makes an encouraging observation about this sort of effort: "In our religious life, passivity comes as the culmination of strenuous activity; passivity without this preliminary condition is sheer inanity" (1952, 276, cited in Fingarette, 1963, 329).

Gradually I came to see that when I was actually able to "do" the practice and be with the counting of the breath, those periods went quickly and effortlessly, with little pain and frustration. I came to see that doing the practice I had been assigned was the path of least resistance away from pain and frustration. I finally learned to allow the breathing process to be. I gradually gave up forcing the body and the breathing into the counting process and no longer mechanically imposed breathing on the body. Just through exhaustion, if nothing else, I came to adopt a more passive attitude to the counting and the breathing, to approximate the appropriate active passivity essential to meditation. In that exhaustion or surrendering of active trying, I began to enter a genuine meditative mood. As one practitioner notes:

I made a great error. It was related to not trying to make it happen. I read a few books on Zen and I knew what was supposed to be happening. So I decided to make it happen. I tried following and counting my breath but nothing would work. Finally I just focused on sound. It was only when I ceased to try to make anything happen that I finally began to develop a practice. Six to eight months [I] was trying to make things happen. Of course, that's what I was doing with my whole life. (no. 58, 3)

As Sudnow notes, scales, chords, and musical theory are the rules that seem in early practice to be the way to jazz improvisation. In fact, however, these ideas give way as the body becomes more skilled in accomplishing movement on the keyboard. In retrospect these early rules and ideas about how jazz improvisation is done come to be seen as entirely inadequate for understanding how the body actually accomplishes the phenomenon. One can no more improvise jazz just knowing musical theory than one can do any highly skilled, embodied activity by just knowing about it. Practice is required. One becomes what one practices. But this practice does not mean imposing the ideas one has about an activity upon the body but, on the contrary, it means allowing the body to come to act and be in a new way. In the Zen setting, what occurs often in the early stages of a beginner's practice is an unlearning of habits of mind and body through a frustration of these habits. The individual finds that meditation simply cannot be done by actively willing it, that is, by using the techniques that seem so often successful in everyday life.

Even this very exhausting work in the early stages had some benefits. It strengthened my diaphragm, deepened my breathing, and reduced the feeling of anxiety that comes from oxygen deprivation. At the same time it exhausted me so that I would often catch a cold at the end of a *sesshin.* I now see this stage of trying as a necessary step that perhaps most beginners go through. For me, it was ultimately a deconditioning, frustrating process, a process that released a lot of anger and attenuated the effort to impose my mental set on the body. Deconditioning is used here to indicate basic alterations in my way of engaging the world that had been learned over a lifetime. In place of these old ways was left an openness that remains unfilled and unformed.

Stage II

Gradually, completing a meditation period of some thirty minutes became less difficult. The muscles stretched, allowing comfort and stability. The body came to be able to assume a position that was previously not achievable, with the spine erect, the lower abdomen tilted slightly forward, the chin tucked in. This stable position is comfortable in itself and provided something that was not available in the beginning, a basis for slowing both physical and mental processes.

This new capability of the body emerged as a discipline; no longer was I tempted continually to itch, flex, or twitch the way, say, a child does. This unthinking moving was diminished by the discipline imposed by the prescriptions for posture and behavior in the zendo that kept the body from intruding on my meditation. The body, once it could assume a more or less comfortable meditative posture, remained nonetheless as a source of pain and tension that I brought to the meditative practice from everyday life. Because I had a nervous stomach, the tension in the abdomen was interfering with my need to relax during meditation (at least I experienced it as such). In this stage the body sits, but still there are the knots left that are carried around day to day.

In this second stage of bodily awareness, I became intimately acquainted with the body as it felt rather than as it looked (imaginatively) in the eyes of others, or in a mirror. There was a definite shift from the body as visualized – a common experience of the body in everyday life – to the body as felt. Pain was central to this process. Regardless of how many years one does sitting meditation, one rarely escapes leg pain completely. It is said among practitioners that the feel of Zen is pain in the knees. During extended periods of meditation this pain can be quite intense, often in subtle ways. As I got more practiced at sitting, I learned to avoid some of the pain by adopting various techniques known to practitioners, including alternating positions from sitting to sitting, avoiding the more demanding positions, and using a variety of pillows to support the legs. As others have pointed out, however, pain can be used to assist meditation (Levine, 1982). What is noticed is the pain can be not only endured but qualitatively changed in terms of how it is experienced. When one relaxes into the pain and does not struggle against it, the pain tends to lessen

A senior monk leading meal chant.

and at times disappears. At best it disappears as suffering. One must, however, glean this through exhaustive efforts.[8]

My experience of the body changed over time into an experience of the bodymind. "The boundary and the battle, between the two has dissolved, a new set of opposites re-united, and a deeper unity discovered. For the first time, you can embody your mind and mind your body" (Wilber, 1979, 120). The more I practiced, the more this experience became a certainty and a fact of my everyday experience as well. Reading Wilber was helpful, of course, in learning to express it in verbal terms.

Stage III

A third stage in bodily awareness emerged as I continued the practice. Both Sekida's (1975) concept of off-sensation and Benoit's (1955) coenaesthesis have drawn attention to this sort of experience. This stage involves a lessening of a separate bodily awareness as the body comes to relax and as bodily tensions are reduced as a result of continual examination by the concentrated mind in meditation. One day I was examining my usual stomach muscle tension in a particularly concentrated way when it seemed to no longer be available as a separate element of my awareness. It disappeared and has never returned, leaving me pleased but somewhat nonplussed by the fact. Practitioners in a variety of meditative and relaxation practices report similar sorts of "healing" experiences.

The body that sits makes possible a stable space in which the mind can examine itself. The body in a good meditative posture all but disappears as a separate sensory input. When the body and mind are in this relaxed modality (inspiring the notion of the relaxation response, according to Benson, 1975), one can watch the interaction between thoughts that come up, having to do with a painful event in the past or uncertainty in the future, and knots in the body. In the midst of this relaxation, tension across the shoulders and in the solar plexus, back of the neck, and the throat can be noticed to appear as thoughts are entertained and can be noticed to disappear as one returns from these thoughts to a meditative posture. It can happen in reverse order as well. Indigestion, strain, and tension in the body can produce scenarios based on memories and fantasies associated with similar bodily states. These can both sustain themselves and provide feedback to amplify the process.[9]

To do the practice is to get the body in a position that allows concentration and relaxation, which permits one to focus on the practice. While sitting *sesshin,* during a sitting period on the third day, I noticed forms taking shape as I gazed at the floor in a rather unfocused fashion. One image came gradually together as a cluster of two or three foxes or some such animal. When I changed my focus or altered my attention, this image changed to just the patterns in the floor. I could go back to the fox image if I wanted to and take a mindtrip. How many foxes are there? What do they mean? What is the symbol of the fox in Japanese culture? Do they have an archetypical meaning in this sense? Or I could notice the image emerging and my mindtrip beginning but then slow or even stop the process. My practice at the time was to follow the breath and review a koan every now and then. When my mind tended to wander, I was to note it, thereby stopping the wandering, for the moment at least. I found on reflection (that is, one of my mind wanderings took the form of reflective thought on the process) that when sufficient skill existed in observing the mind in action, it was possible to choose either to let the mind wander based on the image or simply to follow my breath and let the image fade beyond a veil of nonawareness or nonexistence. Choosing to stay with the practice rather than let the mind wander was a choice, but one that could only be made when there was sufficient ability to concentrate *(samadhi)* to note its emergence. This accumulation of *samadhi* is experienced by practitioners to be linked directly to the duration and intensity of meditative practices.[10]

The person doing Zen meditation is usually familiar with the notion of *hara,* which, in talks given in the zendo, is spoken of as the center of gravity of the body, located just below the navel. It is referred to as the basis of stability, concentration, and enlightened action (Kapleau, 1967, 67–8). Leggett (1978, 87) notes that this concept of a spiritual center of gravity was an element of Taoist teaching in Sung China that was absorbed by the Chan tradition and is common in secular notions of the self in Japan as well.[11] It is this center over which the hands are held in the Zen meditative posture. I was told, "Put your self in your hands." What this meant was for me to focus my concentration in the *hara* where my hands were. When I did this with sufficient concentration, I came to experience an increased stability.

Another instruction was, "Breathe through your heels" – that is, forget about theoretical notions of how breathing is done, just get down into the *hara* area. The heels are very close to the *hara* when one sits in the lotus posture. In this position, focusing on this area, I searched for the body but it simply could not be found. The search entailed not my hands or my imagination but was done in terms of sensory input, of which there was none. I was aware of diffuse energy flows but no feeling that delimited the boundary of body and environment. Focused on the *hara,* unaware of the body as a separate element, I would suddenly become aware of a sound. A car backfiring, a plane overhead, or a bird chirping, for example, was then experienced as "inside" or as "me."

Sitting in such *hara*-focused concentration, I commonly experienced a sound originating in the lower abdomen as a shock wave that existed also in the hands and forearms. This shock is then processed (it seems) through the ears and verbal processes as a particular sound that has an origin some distance outside the house in which I am sitting. The first sensation is a tingling in the *hara* and hands (which remember are held over the *hara*); the second is an upward movement to the head and ears where the sensation is processed into a normalized event by recognizing it as a common form of object or activity.

When I enter a state of meditation even more deeply, I become a sudden noise. Instead of it being centered in the abdomen or expressing itself in the contraction of those muscles with which I often respond to a sudden noise, in meditation there is just the noise. The noise or sound is contained within "me." I do no work, make no effort to accomplish this. This is not a meaning that I learned to do actively. It happens despite me or rather due to my active passivity. I am the sound and that meaning stands whether it is grasped reflexively in so many words or not. The necessary work – hearing with the ears, recognizing the sound as a bird, imagining the house in which I sit and the bird outside – is not done. If this perceptual work of organizing the sound into a world as I and, importantly, others know it to be is not done, if concentration is sufficiently intense so as to slow if not stop this almost automatic perceptual and reality-building process, then it is possible to experience the sound of the bird as being inside oneself. The sounds seem to originate within because there is no awareness of inside–outside, and the theoretical categories and common sense that maintain this boundary are suspended by the meditative state. The sound simply is.

The difficulty of expressing this experience is testified to by one of my informants.

Well you, ah, there's a, after a few days of *sesshin* – you know these terms get thrown around all the time – *samadhi,* ah, well when I really am experiencing what I feel is *samadhi,* then I have a real strong sense of *hara.* I actually, you know, your body just kind of disappears. There's an experience of what's going on. Sometimes I think, well, is it my *hara* now? Where is the experience coming from? I can't really say exactly what it is, where it comes from but, ah, there is that experience and when I'm going through that kind of experience I can focus on my *hara* and just kind of hang there. But that's really all I can say about my experience. (no. 63)

This is a common experience for practitioners as concentration increases and as off-sensation develops. This experience can be extremely important for an individual or it can be without great impact, as in my case. The relevance of such experience for Zen training comes to be established in interaction with a teacher. Such an experience is powerfully important when it is recognized as indicative of one's greater Self, that is the quality of Being that Zen training is facilitating. This glimpse of an alternative way of perceiving is discussed in Chapter VIII. We need to note briefly that such experience is not considered to be a retreat into prerational forms of experience but is in fact quite the opposite. When carried into everyday life beyond the meditative state, it is entirely compatible with a thoroughly practical orientation.

A tape recording was made of awareness in a period of sitting meditation for fifteen minutes. The period spacing between words and phrases indicates relatively the period of time between verbal responses.

There is a slowing down of thinking, a reluctance, a lack of analysis, a lack of verbal stream .... an awareness of sounds, ... feelings .... energy ... down into the *hara* area ... eyes come .... open .... objects noticed .... the breath .... in and out (the voice on the tape recording softens) .... rhythmically .... visual field .... softens ..... no particular objects .... leg, buttocks monitored, no pain .... straighten back, close the *mudra* (hand position) .... energy in the .... lower .... spine .... tension ...... energy ... pleasant .... building to anticipate a climax at a higher level of energy ..... eyes .... cross .... softening of visual field .... awareness of sounds ... mouth drops open ...... pleasant energy in viscera ... eyes close ... return to .... breathing .... pleasant energy across the shoulders and down the spine .... awareness of the center of the forehead, pleasant tension in the center of the forehead .... energy in the viscera .... teeth tend to clench, jaw tightens as the energy flows .... relax .... the jaw .... body boundaries indefinite when reviewed .... can't tell which leg over which leg, can't remember without looking, can't tell by feeling .... can't feel .... indefinite energy not limited to sharp bodily regions ...... energy ..... escaping from the body, from upper torso ... pleasant energy associated with breathing ...... return to breathing .... the koan .... repeat it .... with breathing .... energy coming up as the koan repeats .... middle of the spine behind the solar plexus, in the *hara* area ... feel gooooooooooooood ...... eyes .... crossing .... the .... koan .... takes the attention .... (clock strikes) .... sounds .... breathing .... pleasant .... breathing. eyes open .... shall I stop? ...... is tape running out? .... pleasant energy .... feeling of gratitude .... jaw tightens with energy flowing ...

The telephone rings and the meditation period ends.

This chapter began by noting two common consequences of meditation: an increased ability to concentrate, and deconditioning of the practitioner. The materials of this chapter allow us to understand these claims somewhat better. The practitioner achieves a better ability to concentrate as the body is trained in assuming a comfortable, stable, erect, alert, and attentive position. Off-sensation develops in time so that distractions associated with the body that often interfere with concentration are removed. Also the mind is trained in the process of returning repeatedly to one's practice. Part of Zen meditative practice is becoming aware of the mind's operation, and in this process the practitioner develops an increased ability to see processes of reality construction that were previously just taken for granted and done automatically.

A deconditioning can be seen to occur in the process of meditation to the degree that bodily based sources of habitual action and thought become altered. Such bodily changes occur as reduction of anxiety and increased relaxation develop in the meditative process. The peaks of emotional experience and verbal consciousness are attenuated and stabilized in the meditative practice, and the practitioner comes more and more acquainted with a calm, unhurried, yet practical involvement in the present moment. Rather than merely looking through one's personal and cultural apparatus for reality building, the practitioner comes more and more to look at such an apparatus and thus gain some distance from its automatic enactment.

It is important to see that this practice – that is, the social arrangements of meditative settings and Zen in particular – is not just resocialization in the sense spoken of by socialization theorists and especially constructionist theorists. As has been argued in Chapters V and VI, there is something special about meditative settings that do not allow them to be grasped adequately in such terms. We want to argue explicitly that knowledge and belief are less important than experience in this setting and that concentration (samadhi) states need to be considered in some detail to be adequate to members' experience. What is occurring in meditative settings is not just the resocialization into another form of local knowledge, according to the theories of Geertz and the lifeworld school of phenomenology, but rather the desocialization (to a degree) or deconditioning of practitioners. This process allows an experience of self that is less verbally organized, more absorbed in the immediate present, yet not less effective in the world of practical affairs. This experience, of course, might be seen as a form of local knowledge, but it needs to be understood that this accomplishment is not simply the product of a horizontal translation from one reality to another. Its roots are in processes, practices, and collectively supported interactional forms that take the practitioner "on a path" considerably at odds with those of more conventional realities. The purpose of this book is to expose the special sociological features of such a practice as it exists in a particular kind of meditative setting.

CHAPTER VIII

The Social Organization of Zen Meditative Ritual Practice and Its Consequences

In contrast to the focus in Chapter VII, attention is now turned to some forms of Zen practice that go beyond sitting meditation.[1] The concept of meditation, understood as sitting or resting in most scientific studies of meditation, is extended to something that can be accomplished in action. The highly suggestive work of Bourdieu (1977), Collins (1975, 1981), Goffman (1961), and Wilber (1983), is used to construct a framework for seeing Zen meditative ritual practices as socially organized activities with important consequences for consciousness and behavior. The argument is made that the organization of Zen practice facilitates an experience of reality that is a decided alternative to that reality usually assumed to be typical of everyday life. A general "constructionist" perspective on social reality is used, but it is supplemented by exposing the impact of meditative practices on the individual and the group.

Wilber (1983) recommends this sort of analysis to sociologists as a way of avoiding the limitations of narrowly psychological studies of meditation-related phenomena. We take his suggestion to identify "the fundamental psychosocial relationships constitutive of the contemplative realms" (1983, 126). Although he mentions the importance of the community of practitioners and the relations between student and teacher to this analysis, the analysis in this chapter is limited to the organization of those rituals specifically organized by the occasion called *sesshin,* and an examination of these rituals as the major elements of the Zen environment. The work of Bourdieu (1977) is now briefly reviewed to clarify what is meant by the terms Zen environment and Zen practice in general.

Bourdieu's Concept of Habitus

Bourdieu's *Outline of a Theory of Practice* is a complex work that contains a broad and yet viable scheme for conceptualizing the complexities of the Zen setting. In scope it resembles the popular work of Berger and Luckmann, *The Social Construction of Reality*, but improves on their work considerably by emphasizing the body and its role in understanding human activity as regulated improvisations. This concern with improvisation as a main feature of social life is neglected by most social theories that are based in rationalist, cognitive, or exchange models of social action (Collins, 1975, 1981). It points beyond the notion of self and of rational action as often conceived of in sociology. As complex as these issues are and despite the fact that Bourdieu is not easily summarized, we will deal with his work briefly because it provides a scheme that informs the rest of this study.

For our purposes, Bourdieu's main concepts are those of structure, habitus, and practice.

The structures constitutive of a particular type of environment (e.g. the material conditions of existence characteristic of a class condition) produce *habitus,* systems of durable, transposable *dispositions.* (p. 72)

The habitus could be considered as a subjective but not individual system of internalized structures, schemes of perception, conception, and action common to all members of the same group or class and constituting the precondition for all objectification and apperception. (p. 86)

The habitus ... produces practices which tend to reproduce the regularities immanent in the objective conditions [structures] ... while adjusting to the demands inscribed as objective potentialities in the situation, as defined by the cognitive and motivating structures making up the habitus. (p. 78)

Habitus, or set of dispositions, is for present purposes the most important moment in this dialectical process, and this term is most helpful in our search for a sociological notion of Zen practice. Although habitus seems at first glance to be similar to the typification schemes common to a "lifeworld" *(Lebenswelt)* (Berger & Luckmann, 1966; Schutz, 1967), Bourdieu makes it clear that, although these dispositions indeed have cognitive functions or consequences, they reside in the body – that is, in habits of feeling and acting as well as thinking. This body-based quality of the habitus, formed as it is in an objective environment, is what makes it so useful in considering Zen practice and its consequences. Bourdieu's scheme allows us to begin to think about Zen practice as a body-based training, rooted in experience rather than entirely in either belief or faith (as Wilber, 1983, uses these terms), or in language-based categories for knowing.

Construed in this way, Zen practice is a set of activities done within the objective structures of the Zen environment that contributes to the reshaping of dispositions (habits of feeling, thinking, and acting). This reshaping involves learning that we can call "resocialization," in that one learns how to be a member of the group in the formal sense of the word. This reshaping process allows one to meet behavioral demands of group activities, to recognize the more obvious meanings of theoretical terms used by the group, and so on. However, the process does not stop here; it also involves learning, sometimes called "deconditioning," that alters the way one organizes and experiences the world on very basic levels. Wilson (1984) has argued for the resocialization/deconditioning distinction as a way of understanding the conversion experience found in a yoga group. Although the present analysis of Zen practice differs considerably from his, I agree with his point that one needs to be more sensitive to differences in so-called conversion motifs (Lofland & Skonovd, 1981) among various religious groups and give special attention to socially organized consequences of religious practices that go beyond those normally associated with the term "socialization."

In keeping with Bourdieu, we view such dispositional change as not involving particular forms of action in themselves, just disposition to action. Zen practice, then, does not prescribe how one should act; rather, it alters the habitus or dispositions to act in a particular way, thus providing an alternative to pre-Zen-practice ways of doing.

The particular forms of action that are typical of Zen practitioners are of no special kind; in fact, the Zen tradition emphasizes ordinariness and returning to the marketplace with helping hands upon actualizing enlightenment. What sustains the objective structures of the Zen environment, then, is the practices found within the zendo and within the community of practitioners, especially the relationship between students and teachers.

Let me make this quite clear. The structures of Zen practice do indeed impose definite limits and forms on behavior. For example, *zazen* must be done in particular ways, at particular times, without moving. The schedule of *sesshin* is demanding and explicit and doing it properly takes a serious commitment and self-discipline. Acting in this environment tends to produce a Zen habitus or set of dispositions. Beyond this, there are few if any prescriptions for action. Precepts exist, but they are meant to be taken not as moral prescriptions to guide action but as statements of how one will tend to act under the influence of the Zen habitus (Aitken, 1984; Tipton, 1982).[2]

The way particular practices are accounted for using this scheme is by an interrelating of the objective structures (which produced the dispositions) to the particular situation in which these practices occur. This interrelating of structure and situation usually happens unconsciously. What Bourdieu means by the unconscious is just "forgotten history" or how we have unknowingly been shaped in our dispositions by an environment that was in turn produced by the collective actions of the past.

Habitus then is the mechanism that allows the ongoing production of practices that have what Bourdieu calls "objective meaning." Their meaning is objective because a person's

actions and works are the products of a *modus operandi* of which he is not the producer and has no conscious mastery, they contain an "objective intention" ... which always outruns his conscious intentions. The schemes of thought and expression he has acquired are the basis for the *intentionless invention* of regulated improvisation. (1977, 79)

Although I do not want to argue that forms of spiritual experience and knowledge found in the Zen setting are determined by such structures and practices, I also do not want to argue that the concentrated states of bodymind *(samadhi)* associated with Zen practice (and other similar meditative practices) are entirely independent of such practices. It is precisely the training of the bodymind in the context of the Zen structure that allows the dispositions – defined as schemes of perception, conception, and action common to all members of the same group (Bourdieu, 1977, 86) – to emerge.

Unlike, subjective meaning where one must reflect on experience and relate it to a goal or purpose, objective meaning exists without reflection as the result of the unconscious action of the habitus. "It is because subjects do not, strictly speaking, know what they are doing that what they do has more meaning than they know" (Bourdieu, 1977, 79). One need not deny that subjective meanings exist and originate in a reflexive fashion. However, the notion of objective meanings is that, despite their having no reason or intention on the part of the doer, they are understandable nonetheless. This point is expanded upon in Chapter 9.

This concern with regulated improvisation is particularly apt for the study of Zen settings. One contemporary writer on Zen argues that

zazen praxis is a spiritual discipline whose primary aim is to explore the nonintentional dimension of consciousness, in which the 'subject' is active as pure Awareness without 'intending' anything, instead of acting as 'subject' as opposed to 'object'. (Izutsu, 1982, 77)

Bourdieu's ability to address such activity theoretically makes his work, when appropriately qualified and articulated with the work of Sudnow, Goffman, Collins, and Wilber, particularly helpful in our analysis. All of these writers allow us to take as a sociological topic human activity that usually falls through the net of social theory – namely, conduct that is recognizable by members as appropriate but cannot be understood either as the product of the rational, calculating intentions of the actor or as mechanistically produced reflections of a deeper social structure.[3]

By following the regimen of a Zen group with its organized activities found in the zendo and during *sesshin*, a member does Zen practice. This is to say that a member practices doing those activities of Zen structure (*zazen* and the many other associated rituals, including work practice). To the extent that one practices diligently and continuously on such structures, a habitus (set of dispositions) develops that influences one to act in certain ways that are recognizably Zenlike. This claim is supported by a variety of research done on meditation in general.[4]

To reveal the influence of Zen ritual practice on the practitioner, the arrangements of *sesshin* will be treated as a Zen environment. The argument is made that *sesshin* arrangements and the ritual activities that occur therein, when practiced with sufficient intensity and persistence, tend to produce a set of dispositions for acting, feeling, and thinking (or not thinking) that are typical of the group of people who are influenced by such an environment, namely Zen practitioners. By participating in *sesshin*, practitioners are put in an environment different in very identifiable ways from that of their everyday lives (recall the social homogeneity of Zen practitioners). The tension created in this process between Zen and non-Zen arrangements for the maintenance of self allows for the possibility of self-change and an alternative experience of reality.

Ritual, Self-Transformation, and Reality Construction

The importance of ritual can be seen in Goffman's work. He has argued that ritual training is an important mechanism whereby a society produces in its members the minimal requirements for living with others. Self, pride, dignity, and tact are all learned and manifested in ritual practices and become the basis for what is perceived as human nature.

Universal human nature is not a very human thing. By acquiring it, the person becomes a kind of construct, built up not from inner psychic propensities but from moral rules that are impressed upon him from without. These rules, when followed, determine the evaluation he will make of himself and of his fellow participants in the encounter, the distribution of his feelings, and the kinds of practices he will employ to maintain a specified and obligatory kind of ritual equilibrium. The general capacity to be bound by moral rules may well belong to the individual, but the particular set of rules which transforms him into a human being derives from requirements established *in the ritual organization of social encounters*. (Goffman, 1967, 44–45, quoted in Collins, 1980, 179; emphasis added)

While this notion of human nature is not in complete agreement with that implicit in the present study, Goffman's clear statement of the relationship between ritual and the learning of basic ways of being human is quite helpful for our purposes. It provides a context for appreciating the consequences of ritual practices in a Zen setting. Because Goffman has already examined some features of monastic settings in this fashion, and because the ritual organization of Zen practice in one of the settings that we are considering is nearly identical to Zen monastic organization, we now turn to a brief summary of this analysis. First, however, a definition of meditative ritual and its place in Zen practice is needed.

When we look closely at the practices of so-called new religious forms, especially Eastern religious forms, we notice that only certain kinds of rituals are present. Bird (1978, 176–7) finds few rituals that deal, among other things, with confession or penance, or with the ordering of social relationships; instead, therapeutic, meditational, and initiatory rituals predominate. Zen groups are generally recognized as sects of Buddhism that emphasize meditative practices almost exclusively as the means to enlightenment. Consequently, my concern will be limited to meditative ritual practices and the implications they have for self-change and conversion. One might well argue, of course, that therapeutic or socially integrating consequences also result from these practices. The point here is merely that meditative rituals are central in the groups studied and merit attention.

Meditative ritual refers to an organized set of activities that are done approximately the same way every time, are valued in themselves, and, when done properly, both require and produce a state of concentration and alertness.[5] For the purposes of this chapter, they are special activities that occur in or near a meditation hall during the special occasion called *sesshin.* It is also assumed that other meditative ritual practices are done in conjunction with sitting. The specifics of such ritual in the *sesshin* setting are now considered.

Goffman's analysis of total institutions in *Asylums* (1961) is well known. He deals with the mechanisms used by monasteries, asylums, prisons, and similar institutions to make changes in new members, so as to guarantee the institution's smooth operation and ultimately to produce the kinds of persons they find desirable. He argues there are some basic practices involving strong social controls that he calls "mortification procedures," that have the result of modifying the self of the inmate by destroying the basis upon which the old, and now undesirable, self existed. From his point of view, the self, then, can be seen as

something that resides in the arrangements prevailing in a social system for its members. The self in this sense is not a property of the person to whom it is attributed, but dwells rather in the pattern of social control that is exerted in connection with the person by himself and those around him. This special kind of institutional arrangement does not so much support the self as constitute it. (Goffman, 1961, 108)

This limited notion of the self concept[6] can be used very effectively to see some of the consequences of doing Zen ritual practice.

Goffman's mortification processes include limiting interaction with others to the inmate role, obedience tests that involve physical abuse and humiliation, elimination of personal property and privacy, and, in general, removal of all possibilities for autonomy. These procedures are a way of controlling others so as to alter the basis on which a particular form of self is constructed, regardless of what kind it is. Whether it is a deviant self in the case of those suffering from the contingencies of being labeled "criminal" or "mentally ill," or simply an inappropriate self in the case of recruits to whaling ships or the military, or even voluntary participants in monastic settings, all are seen as socially malleable. Common to all these settings are certain practices and arrangements that facilitate the reconstruction of a self.

The *sesshin* period in Zen settings can be seen in a similar fashion. *Sesshin* is a period of intensive, collective practice usually ranging from three to seven days and nights. It centers around a zendo (meditation hall) in which a Zen teacher and the voluntary participants carry out the prescribed ritual activities. Usually dormitory facilities are available, often of a very primitive sort, which allows participants to stay physically close to the zendo and in this way stay involved even during periods of rest. A typical daily schedule for a *sesshin* is as follows:

9:30 P.M. lights out

4:00 A.M. wake up
4:30 A.M. sitting meditation in zendo
6:00 A.M. service (chanting, bowing, etc.)
7:00 A.M. formal breakfast ritual in zendo

7:45 A.M. break
8:15 A.M. work period
10:30 A.M. sitting meditation in zendo
12:00 service
12:30 P.M. formal lunch ritual in zendo
1:15 P.M. break
2:30 P.M. sitting meditation in zendo
3:00 P.M. talk by teacher
4:00 P.M. sitting meditation in zendo

4:30 P.M. service
5:00 P.M. informal evening meal and break
6:30 P.M. sitting meditation in zendo
9:00 P.M. end sitting
9:30 P.M. lights out

4:00 A.M. wake up

Beginners often find some basic rules and arrangements of *sesshin* mortifying. Participants:

1. usually sleep on the floor in sleeping bags in rather crowded conditions;
2. share bathroom facilities that are crowded, and must cue up for them;
3. are restricted from taking showers and baths for the duration (for practical, not theoretical, reasons);
4. are not allowed to break the demanding schedule to suit personal whims;
5. are instructed to avoid distracting personal expressions such as bright or revealing clothing, jewelry, or perfume;

A senior student walks slowly around the zendo with a *kyasaku* (stick) that is used to give a stimulating blow on the muscles of the upper back to those who request it.

6. take collective meals that are often quickly paced and do not allow idiosyncratic eating habits;
7. are expected to maintain prescribed hand postures both in and out of the zendo for the duration of *sesshin;* and
8. are expected to do full bows (prostrations) with others during particular rituals.

These few arrangements in themselves are enough to introduce considerable frustration and annoyance into the lives of most beginners. If one is seriously committed to keeping these rules – and as we will see, it is difficult to stay in *sesshin* and not do so – surprising changes in the way one experiences oneself and the world can occur. These are only the most basic sorts of behavioral demands made by the organization of *sesshin.* Many more precise prescriptions for ritual performance exist as well. *Sesshin* is a tightly organized social setting in which behavioral demands increase in subtlety as one's skill in doing them develops. Thus the more senior participants as well as beginners feel a strong change in experience. This is especially true because, as Goffman correctly points out, participants in religious institutions give themselves to these practices with surprising energy in an effort to accomplish the goals of the practice (typically termed "enlightenment" in this setting).

To show how easy it might be for *sesshin* participants to find these arrangements mortifying, consider how many Americans shower every day, wash their hair at least every other day, and expect immediate access to elaborate, private toilet facilities. As Goffman argues, our selves are constituted by these (and other) conveniences. If there is not an attachment to the bathroom, others of us have strong habits associated with eating; we have fixed notions of what we can eat, how much is appropriate, how fast we can eat, in what order, and so forth. Other demands of the schedule may also produce frustrating circumstances: not enough rest, not the right kind of work assigned during work periods, sitting in a part of the zendo that is drafty, or sitting next to the wrong person. For others it is the postures prescribed for the hands or the bowing that may remind them of their earlier (e.g., Catholic) selves – acts that can be exceedingly mortifying to recall and enact.

While these may seem trivial in the abstract, for those who encounter these arrangements for the first time, the impact is usually strong enough to move them into a modified experience of self where the question of who they are and what they are doing cannot simply be taken for granted. This mood fits nicely with the wider practices and goals of *sesshin.* A monk states that when he first came up to the Los Angeles Center,

I was suspicious that they were going to ... [unclear verb meaning "take"] my money. Then after the first *sesshin* here I got enough of an experience of it, of the *it*, to know that all the stuff they were saying in the books and in the zendo wasn't bullshit. (no. 32, 7)

Thus far, the logic has been identical to Goffman's. We have emphasized how controls different from the usual context of self can produce a change in self, if ever so briefly. In *Asylums*, Goffman discusses how the inmate "makes out" in these uncongenial settings by withholding commitment in practices he calls "secondary adjustments." These practices allow the individual to find some basis of self-respect and autonomy by resisting officially prescribed ways of being while still behaving appropriately.[7] Although this analysis is brillant, it does not apply particularly well to the current setting, primarily because participation in the Zen setting is voluntary. If students feel the need to resist strongly, they can simply leave. However, although some do leave for various reasons, most practitioners do their best to give themselves more and more to the practice as a way of squelching that self that tries to survive by resisting. Specifically, Goffman notes that antagonism or unconcern are symbols of self-determination and of efforts to resist the new social conditions. One seldom sees antagonism or unconcern in the zendo and, when seen, they always involve the beginner who has not yet been able to accept fully the demands of the practice.[8]

As was seen in Chapter VII, considerable social pressure exists to maintain at least external conformity to behavioral demands and to avoid any visible expression of resistance or affectation. Participation in the rituals of Zen practice, especially during *sesshin* periods, contributes directly to the attenuation of the practices that constitute self in everyday life. Although the impact of such arrangements might seem trivial, when one adds to these arrangements the impact of rising at 4:00 A.M., sitting for hours in a physically demanding posture, forgoing diversions, and maintaining silence for a period of three, five, or even seven days at a time, the potential impact of *sesshin* appears more credible.

Goffman, of course, is not the only theorist who offers help in understanding the impact of ritual practice on an experience of self and reality. If we shift our focus from the "conditions" that Goffman argues constitute the self to interactional practices and reflexive processes used by actors to produce a sense of shared reality, we can better see how Zen practitioners go about experiencing "Zen reality." This shift allows us to avoid the problem of over objectifying the environment in which Zen practice occurs and the so-called reality experienced therein.

Tart (1975) has already begun such an analysis by suggesting that Zen practice, among other techniques of spiritual psychologies, influences the mental functioning of individuals and the production of altered states of consciousness, a point that can be modified somewhat to suit our interests. The impact of the practice needs to be considered not only as altered states but also as practical and healthful – that is, consequences that can be seen clearly within ordinary consciousness. Examples are obvious and include the reduction of anxiety, improved muscle balance and posture, and the reduced dominance of the verbal consciousness. Also, and more important, the body becomes trained largely in what might be considered normal consciousness, at least at first, if one takes Sudnow's experience as an exemplar. However, as practice continues, just as in Sudnow's case, the entire body begins to take on ways of being and acting that are not entirely those intended by the "speaking I." Finally, the body comes to develop ways of being and acting that are not totally separated from the I but that this I seems merely to witness. Another way of describing this phenomenon is by reference to the bodymind, as discussed in Chapter VII. This emphasis on Sudnow's approach replaces somewhat the value of ritual as a concept for analysis. Sudnow's description points to the elements of ritual activities on a more basic or grounded level. Ritual does not cease to be important; rather, the way it is examined and described is, for us, grounded in an analysis and description of its impact on both the body and mind. My approach draws on the work of symbolic interactionists, phenomenological perspectives associated with Schutz, and the ritual theory of Durkheim and Collins.

In the following analysis, I am not seeking to identify just language-based, reality-building practices, but rather an interactional organization that supports certain activities and discourages others; facilitates the channeling of energies into activities that tend to attenuate typical (everyday) practices, sensitivities, and assumptions; and positively produces and supports alternative sorts of experiences and bodymind modalities.

Five main consequences of the social organization of Zen ritual practice will be analyzed. These consequences are a reduction of self-consciousness; a lowering of the level of reflexivity; a retraining of attention; an increase in concentration; and collective stimulation and support for individual practice. With these points in mind, let us turn to an analysis of how Zen ritual practice facilitates new sorts of experience.

Reduction of Self-Consciousness

Zen practice is organized to facilitate a reduction of self-consciousness. The *sesshin* setting differs from Goffman's analysis in an important way. Little if any confrontation occurs between staff and practitioners, with one or two ritual exceptions that will be mentioned later. As noted elsewhere, deviations from behavioral prescriptions are corrected only well after the fact and in a fashion that is impersonal. In fact, there is no public shaming in the zendo (a feature that may be typical of other monastic settings). The Zen setting tends to avoid all practices in the zendo that encourage self-consciousness, whether these practices are positive or negative in content. Thus, any confrontation, criticism, or approval is usually avoided. This approach eliminates a source of unsolved problems and a preoccupation with self that tend to remain with the person as sources of anxiety.

Reduced Reflexivity

Zen practice facilitates an altered experience of reality by providing an organized context for reduced reflexivity. The most basic rules of *sesshin* that immediately begin to disrupt a sense of life as usual by reducing normal reflexive activity are:

1. No talking. Silence is to be maintained at all times except in some few special situations, and then talk is in a whisper. If we consider the role of talk in sociological theories of consensus building, this is no small break with the normal reflexive mechanisms for reality construction.
2. No social greetings necessary. No thank you, good morning, please, after you, or gestures indicating as much. This effectively removes a layer of normal diplomatic interaction rituals and allows one to relax out of the attention given to the normal set of social obligations. Attention can now be focused elsewhere.
3. No looking around. Keep the eyes down at about a forty-five-degree angle at all times. This further limits social obligations but more importantly severely limits the relevance of and stimulation by those objects and events that normally hold our attention. Observing this rule takes practice and commitment, but it is amazingly effective for reducing thought processes.
4. No writing, reading, radio, television.
5. Hold hands in *shashu* (the right hand held over the left hand, which is held in a fist over the solar plexus) when not in otherwise prescribed position. This procedure does reminds one that *sesshin* is a special time and place, and reminds others as well. If the hands are not held in this position, it is clear sign of lapses of concentration.
6. No individual deviation from the *sesshin* schedule. Get up when the bell rings. Do what is scheduled when the event is announced. Do not anticipate it, do not get up early or late. To innovate is "extra" and is conducive to and indicative of usual self practices. No special plans or arrangements are necessary or allowed. Just keep the schedule.

The unusual nature of the *sesshin* occasion is clear. It provides a nonproblematic setting where one can concentrate on what is called one's "practice," or the focused observation of the mind in operation. All other concerns are simplified or eliminated. The rules allow all participants to agree ahead of time what will be done, who will do it, and how. No special negotiations are necessary on the meaning of self, other, situation. All is clear, repetitious, simple. My view that this has an impact upon the self is supported by a contemporary social psychologist's thinking as well.

Self-reflective behavior is variable in its occurrence in interaction. In the philosophic point of view from which symbolic interactionism derives, thinking occurs as a response to a problematic situation. The self-reflective activity labeled "self" is a form of thinking. The implication is clear: where situations are totally unproblematic (perhaps a rare event in modern society), there may be no self. (Stryker, 1980, 58)

(That the self goes beyond just cognitive or thinking operations is something that Stryker also notes and with which I readily agree.)

By practicing in this unusual setting, one acquires experience in a way of being with others and oneself that is, in terms of reality-construction practices, considerably different from everyday life. It is not uncommon for a participant to conclude a seven-day *sesshin* without ever having seen the eyes of the other participants (with the exception of the teacher in private interviews), or for that matter ever having seen much above their waist. Even after spending long days in closely organized interaction with other members, they remain largely amorphous and devoid of particular visual features. This lack of common visual–social stimulation, coupled with the observing of silence for this period, is a most unusual experience in our society. When combined with the other ritual practices and sitting meditation, the impact on the person can be very powerful.

For the beginner, *sesshin* can provide a temporary but potentially important experience of self and reality far removed from the everyday. The controls exerted by others and by oneself in the *sesshin* setting are the mechanism for the production of this new experience. With very little visual input from others' faces, talk, and clothing, there is little stimulation of the reflexive processes on self–other themes and relevancies so typical of everyday life. Reflexive processes that do occur tend to center around the themes and materials that are relevant to one's practice (e.g., counting the breath). When done long enough, intensively enough, and with sufficient diligence, this practice can have a drastic temporary, and sometimes lasting, influence on the person. (One teacher speaks of the impact of *sesshin* as the pushing through of walls and glimpsing the possibilities of awareness in states of *samadhi*. Because these walls have not yet been removed, however, one needs to practice, or consciousness soon returns to the pre-*sesshin* state.)

Retraining of Attention

Zen practice facilitates an altered experience of reality by a retraining of attention. As discussed in Chapter VII, accepting an attitude of active passivity is essential to the meditative experience. More than an attitude or psychological stance, it is a stance that tends to be built into the social organization of Zen practice in that any other attitude tends to be counter-productive. On the one hand, trying to "do" meditation with the engaged, purposive will typical of everyday life leads to frustration and failure in the way discussed in Chapter VII. On the other hand, the arrangements of *sesshin* are such that it is extremely difficult to act in bad faith – that is, to be in *sesshin* for five to seven days and not participate in it with dedication, diligence, and sincerity. The positions inevitably produce pain. Schedules tend to be so simple, lacking in possibilities for entertainment and diversion, that if participants do not enter into them in good faith and actually begin to accomplish the states of concentration available through the practice, they are left bored and daydreaming, and ultimately unable to tolerate the demands of the schedule. It exaggerates the pain. Persons who attempt to cheat, to do what Goffman calls "spiritual leave-taking," find themselves confronted with an untenable situation that is painful, boring, and frustrating, hour after hour. The Zen practitioner must find the appropriate way for "doing" meditative rituals somewhere be-tween cheating by doing something else and doing too much. Some never do find this way and drop out. Because this attitude bears on the next element that facilitates an alternative experience in a Zen setting, con-centration, this discussion will be continued under that heading.

Increased Concentration and Alertness

Zen practice facilitates an altered experience of reality through increased concentration and alertness. At the core of Zen practice is the training of the ability to attend to the elements of consciousness. How this occurs in *zazen* has been examined in Chapters V and VII; the other rituals of Zen practice are addressed in this section with the same interest in mind.

Schutz (1967) has developed the notion of "finite provinces of mean-ing," similar to James's subuniverses of reality, as a way of dealing with the great variety of human experience. He considers the reality of every-day life to be paramount. All other provinces of meaning are less central and differ in terms of their cognitive style. As examples of nonparamount realities, he lists the worlds of dreams, artistic experience, religious ex-perience, scientific contemplation, child's play, and the insane. These realities are constituted by the actor entering into the cognitive modality that is particular to each one. The main characteristics of Zen meditation can be considered in terms of this scheme of the cognitive constitution of meaning but at a certain cost. If one allows Schutz's cognitive scheme to determine one's perspective on Zen practice, some other less cognitive dimensions of this setting are missed that are most interesting. Schutz can be used, however, to examine the role played by an alternative form of attention in the Zen setting.

Schutz finds each form of reality or "finite province of meaning" constituted by (among other things) what he calls "a specific tension of consciousness." He finds everyday reality as being most "wide-awake" in this regard because it "originates in an attitude of 'full attention' to life and its requirements" (Schutz, 1967, 212). This involves a form of active attention in which the meanings of objects are considered in terms of a pragmatic frame of reference.

Another constitutive element of each reality is "a specific form of experiencing oneself." In everyday realities, Schutz argues, the working self is the total self. "Only the performing [thinking] and especially the working self is fully interested in life and, hence, wide-awake" (1967, 213). He notes further that "the working self experiences itself as the originator of the ongoing actions" (1967, 216). Because Schutz takes the pragmatic relevancies and the active engagement of the body in the world of everyday life as basic and paramount, any reality that is different from this is, by definition, less wide-awake. He finds scientific theorizing, for example, and the attitude of the disinterested observer to be less awake in this regard. The modality of the attention essential for meditation would no doubt force him to treat this as less awake as well.[9]

By considering just these two points from a much longer discussion of this perspective by Schutz, an examination of Zen ritual practices shows how attention and experience of self differ. I hope to show how an alternative experience to that of everyday life is facilitated by the social organization of Zen practice and more specifically by the cultivation of unusual levels of concentration.[10]

Beginning Zen practice, the practitioner usually has little ability to concentrate and is not familiar with the details of Zen ritual, which necessitates continual self-conscious monitoring of performance. The body is being trained to do certain postures and movements, and the demands on hands, eyes, and the body as a whole are complex enough to demand close, active attention. One of the most demanding rituals, *oryoki,* or formal meals in the zendo, usually takes long practice before the novice becomes competent. Regular practice leads to increasing familiarity and ease in doing all the rituals, however, and gradually permits a less self-conscious involvement.

Sitting meditation is the core of Zen practice, and the practice one is assigned by the teacher is the key device for training. Beginners working on counting the breath, for example, are encouraged to work on this even while doing other rituals (and in break periods, for that matter). The ability to observe the mind in operation gradually improves with diligent effort and long practice so that, while one is involved in any activity, the practitioner is constantly striving to maintain this state. This task is difficult, however, and certain ritual occasions offer materials for noticing the limits of one's abilities.

Some beginners have strong aversion to some ritual forms, like bowing or holding the hands in the position the Japanese call *gassho.* A common sentiment is, "I'll sit but I won't do that other hocus-pocus." The problem is that there is strong social pressure (however subtle) in the zendo to conform closely to ritual prescriptions. Refusal to do the offensive ritual is noticed and makes the beginner uncomfortable, whereas doing it brings frustration and even what Goffman calls mortification. Usually, the person participates in the ritual, and the emotion and thoughts associated with it gradually diminish. No new interpretation is provided in place of the old one, at least not officially. The old meaning (emotions, ideas) just fades in doing the ritual over and over again. Practice comes to attenuate, diminish, and transform emotions and ideas and leaves just the doing in their place.

Even though ritual practice continues to be demanding even for more senior students, beginners come to experience some confidence in doing it. With practice one finds the appropriate state of actively passive attention and lets behavior move along prescribed lines. Because the rituals have been done repeatedly, the body becomes trained. As concentration increases during *sesshin,* the practitioner capably meets most ritual demands. The result is less stumbling and greater competence and confidence in both ritual and nonritual settings (Tipton, 1979, 292).

A beginner soon begins to grasp, however, that it is not one's usual self or awareness that is responsible for the success in doing. One senses what Sudnow calls a "mysterious achievement," and notices that the normal verbal and purposive self actually interferes with an adequate performance. This self leads to stumbling and the missing of cues. Self-confidence increases as one's skill and concentrative ability increase, but it is confidence based in trust in a self or character that is "beyond" or "below" the verbal self – a self that verbal awareness can only partially sense and that appears much more "natural" in retrospect. One reason for this is simply that it includes capabilities of the body that the verbal self previously imagined that it somehow controlled but in ritual practice does not initiate. This perception of self and its importance is noted to occur in other settings as well (Csikszentmihalyi, 1975; Messinger, Sampson, & Towne, 1962; Suzuki, 1959). Similar observations about the importance of the body and its relation to an alternative sense of self can be found in James (1890, 301), Merleau-Ponty (1962, 206), and Polanyi (1967, 15–16).[11]

A practitioner gradually develops the skills to do the expected behavior and in time comes to do it without reflection – without judgments, comparisons, or pride. What one learns is a role (expected behavior) certainly, but only to the beginner or observer in a reflexive posture, not to the accomplished doer. To the doer it is just activity that is smooth, coordinated, effortless, and conscious but not self-conscious. As soon as one's attention strays, however, so does performance, and one feels immediately that the activity is in error and inappropriate.

Chanting is an example of ritual feedback. An individual can do it alone as if he or she were the only person doing it, putting emphasis on reading or saying each syllable correctly. In this case it is not unusual for self-consciousness to interfere with the successful performance of the chant. This self-consciousness can vary from anticipation of errors or worrys about past errors to pride in accomplishment. Each causes stumbling in the chant. Chanting passively ("chant with your ears," one is told) – listening to others, following their lead and their pace, letting them cue you to the next syllable – leads to effective performance. When smoothness in this form of ritual is experienced, the individual self or verbal consciousness is seen as less effective than awareness of the group process. Whether this fact is recognized or not has little if anything to do with its reality. Behavior is changed.

As a beginner develops the ability to act competently in a ritual such as chanting, there are opportunities to become more involved by learning more demanding and specialized activities. The role of chant leader *(ino)*, for example, involves a set of activities that must be done (i.e., sung) solo. The greater detail in the task and its "fateful" quality owing to its individualized nature provides the person who practices it renewed feedback on one's fears, insecurities, and, finally, capabilities, as one's self-confidence grows through the development of skills and successful performance. The goal is not just competence, however, but what Benedict (1946, 235) has called "expertness" and others call enlightenment.

This same feedback occurs in other rituals as well. After about thirty minutes of sitting meditation, a bell is rung, and all participants rise slowly, stand facing the center, and in a definite and specified way, punctuated by the sound of wooden clappers and bells, do about five minutes of walking meditation *(kinhin)*. Even this respite from the physical strain of sitting is structured to demand close attention. At the sound of wooden clappers, all bow slightly and turn to the left; another clap sounds to mark the beginning of a slow walk. One small step is taken slowly for every complete cycle of breathing. After a minute or so another clap sounds

Participants doing outside walking meditation (*kinhin*). Wooden clappers used to signal phases of the meditation are seen here carried at the ready by the leader.

the beginning of a faster walk. Participants are instructed to "stay close to the one in front of you," and often there is a need to adjust one's pace as the circle of walkers alternately bunches up and flows again. A clap sounds, all stop at their places and turn to the center; a bell sounds, and all bow and turn to sit and begin the next thirty-minute period of sitting. No opportunity for breaking concentration is intended.

As in the case of chanting, feedback is immediate because rituals for the most part are highly choreographed actions. If one breaks concentration, behavior is quickly atypical. Perhaps it is no more than walking on the heels of the person in front or turning in one direction as all turn in the other. This feedback comes directly and unambiguously, and sooner or later it is seen by the individual as the result of being in verbal consciousness. As soon as a person begins to think, daydream, or focus on a detail of the process in an effort to anticipate behavioral demands, appropriate behavior becomes increasingly difficult.

Rituals of communal meals taken during *sesshin* involve quite a complicated behavioral process punctuated by chanting, wooden clappers, and drums. As in all of zendo practices, there is pressure to conform rather closely to the timing and movements of the whole group. All face the middle and have good peripheral vision of others' movements. There is room, of course, for individual pacing in the actual eating stage, but preparation and cleaning of the bowls *(oryoki)* are closely coordinated processes. When a participant is relaxed and passively attentive, all sorts of cues, assists, and complementary movements are available that allow the appropriate activity to be accomplished. Only when one moves into verbal consciousness, private concerns, and dreams that are so typical of everyday consciousness, does the action stumble and even freeze. The consequences of this practice (and one is not taught this specifically) are a gradual identification of a smooth "performance" as being done, or better, witnessed, by one's actively attentive self, and a recognition that what interferes with smooth action is the reflecting and limited verbal consciousness.

Collective Stimulation and Support

Zen practice facilitates an altered experience of reality by the use of collective stimulation and support. The social pressures, rooted in a strong identification with others, are considerable. These pressures pull people into commitments to the practice that they would not otherwise make, or if made, would not be able to keep on their own. For example, the person who is unwilling to move during a sitting period, who is unwilling to violate the rule to not move and thus disturb others close by, endures tremendous pain and frustration in order not to violate the group expectations.

The only reason I stayed is because people next to me [in the zendo] were staying.

One can always do just one more second, one more breath. (no. 12 in dharma talk)

The consequences of this attitude are curious. A person's commitment to a particular kind of self-structure – I am independent, strong, willful, and the kind of person who can do it – inadvertently forces one into a crucible of experience in which insight into the limits of this self is possible. The frustrating self-confrontations that one would otherwise never allow are tolerated and lived through in the name of the very self that is being exposed, in the experience of sitting, as "illusory." Collective practice uses self-energy, ego energy, and mechanisms that function to maintain particular identities and ideologies to erode this same self (or at least to diminish the ability to identify with it) and to expose the self to contradictions and potential insights. Equally important, the energies produced in collective practice provide an experience of body and mind that is often described as stable, calm, concentrated, and alert.

A *sesshin* tends to generate energy both on an individual and collective level as it proceeds. Various insider notions address this common experience of stages of *sesshin.* The briefest *sesshin,* usually lasting two or three days is spoken of as being all work and pain. Just as the body adjusts to the demands of the extended sitting schedule, it is over. A *sesshin* lasting five or seven days is spoken of, sometimes in awe by beginners, as not as painful after the third day, involving deep concentration possibilities, and sometimes as being disorienting (the head of the woodworking shop, for example, once told me he tries to keep people from using the power saws after the fifth day). Teachers regularly speak of the "strength" of a *sesshin,* of participants settling down or in, and of concentration developing in the zendo as a whole. How can this accumulation of energy be seen as related to the social organization of ritual practices and as facilitating an alternative experience?

Sociologically, the most obvious way to understand the accumulation of energy is to use Durkheim's (1965) theory of ritual.[12] Collins (1975) has provided us with a summary of Durkheim's theory of ritual that lets us see immediately why energy would be expected to increase in a zendo setting.

To do religion is to create a mood and a belief, to call forth a Holy Spirit. How is this done? It requires, first of all, *a group of people, concentrating their attention* in such a way as to generate a common mood and a common object of thought. There must be no individual concerns apart from the group, no side conversations or activities. The physical setting is structured to enhance this mood and to avoid distraction; hence, ... The group's *actions are stereotyped* in some degree, whether these are ritual gestures or verbal formulas.... The stereotyping may be seen as an aid to concentrating everyone's attention, evoking a single definition of reality and *a mutually reinforced emotion....* Finally, there is the name or other symbol for the spirit invoked; this makes the transient mood into a visitation of something more permanent and recallable. (Collins, 1975, 94–95; emphasis altered)

Both Collins and Durkheim are concerned with the impact of such rituals on collective consciousness and social solidarity. In a statement that is almost brutal, Collins makes this point: "Interaction also serves as a machine for intensifying emotion and for generating new emotional tones and solidarities" (Collins, 1981, 1001). There are problems with this concept, however, when applied to meditative settings. To examine these problems will take us closer to details of our particular research setting and show again how it differs from other more typical ritual occasions.

Although a variety of difficulties in applying Durkheim's and Collins' schemes to a Zen setting can be found, I will here address only the one that is most central, namely, the problem of treating collective energies as "emotional" energy. What is emotional energy? For Collins (1981), in social interaction "the stronger the common emotional tone, the more real the invoked topic [of conversation] will seem to be and the greater the solidarity in the group" (p. 1001). One who is accepted into the interaction "acquires an increment of positive emotional energy ... what we commonly call confidence, warmth, and enthusiasm" (pp. 1001–1002). Although there is a range of emotional energies, Collins emphasizes those associated with feelings of solidarity – trust, acceptance, liking, or the lack of these. These feelings are involved in coalition formation and membership, his major interest. One could do an analysis of meditative groups in this fashion, and Wilber (1983) outlines the concern with legitimacy of social arrangements in such groups as an important sociological topic; however, it would be an error to take these sorts of "energies" as the only kinds that are relevant in our setting. Emotions can be profitably differentiated from "feelings," or what is sometimes referred to as "hedonic tone." Whereas the word "emotions" is illustrated by such things as fear, love, hate, joy, sadness, melancholy, and bliss, "feelings" indicates experiences of pleasure or discomfort associated with our perceptions such as tension, pain, relaxation, energetic states, calmness, stability, and lightness (Johansson, 1969, 24).

This second category of "feelings" is most salient in a discussion of

Zen practice. This is not to say that Collins' notion of emotional energies is incorrect. Rather I want to argue that although emotions can be modulated by collective practices and vary throughout one's career in Zen practice (see Brown, 1977, for the variable and nonspecific relationship between cognitive and emotional experiences in a concentrative meditation practice), they remain less relevant for a description of Zen experience than do a form of feelings that are associated historically with meditative practices, namely, spiritual energies.[13]

The word spiritual is used here not to refer to any other-worldly entities but to human capabilities that can be spoken of as clearly as we speak of the emotions. One difficulty, however, is that at least the more common emotions are available in everyday life without needing to stimulate or cultivate them using special practices. Spiritual energies, especially in a materialist epoch, often are not present or not recognized as such if present. Not only do sensate cultures such as those in the United States and Western Europe tend to label such energies in nonspiritual ways with the result they become experienced and treated as symptoms of mental or physical disturbance (cf. Laing's *The Politics of Experience*), but industrial sensate cultures even tend to destroy the more common practices and ways of life that facilitate the production of such energies. (The emphasis put upon the verbal modality in industrial societies and the distractions provided by a technologically expanded environment are two examples of this destructive tendency.) Japan is an exception to this trend and has maintained much of its traditional culture, despite industrialization. There, a ready acceptance of spiritual energies is found as an important dimension of everyday life (Lebra, 1976, 159). One finds this same acceptance among practitioners of Zen in this country.

The kind of spiritual energy with which we are concerned is that associated with *hara.* The martial arts perhaps represent the clearest common social form that is based in this bodymind modality. The other so-called *do* or ways also recognize and teach the embodiment of such a sensitivity (Suzuki 1959). This sensitivity is easily missed by those unacquainted with it. Although it has been written of in the various religious and philosophic traditions of Asia, this sensitivity is usually perceived by outsiders as no more than a curious typification of experience, which is at worst superstitious and at best nothing more than common experience found in everyday life in their own culture. Few social scientists have taken these accounts seriously. One suspects that we have ignored them because they seem to us unreal, because we do not experience them in our everyday or even special experience. Those who have reported them as Westerners have been able to do so because they have entered them as more than observers. Only by doing so is contact with the bodymind modality, referred to here, genuinely made.

This point is worth making because sociologists understand ritual practices as generating energies of solidarity, warmth, and enthusiasm, which are considered, properly I think, to be emotional energies. Meditative settings, however, produce spiritual energies in ritual processes that contribute to solidarity but take the form of calmness, stability in the face of sudden stimulation, and ability to attend and to concentrate on what is present and to act appropriately (von Duerckheim, 1977, 49–51). These energies can be felt most certainly but are directly related to cognitive processes as well. Thus, they are referred to as states of body-mind and as the Zen "habitus." Not only is the body calm and stable, the mind as well in this state is unmoving, not reflecting, and seemingly directly in touch with present exigencies.

A school of thought in psychology sees emotions closely related to facial expression. Izard (1977), taking this position, argues that a particular emotion can be felt when the proper facial posture is taken. Regardless of the validity of this claim, the face clearly can reveal feelings. The facial expression sometimes associated with strong spiritual energies is staring small pupils, with the mouth set and its corners turned down. The look might be described as fierce, but in my experience it is related to strong tension and energy in the *hara*; in fact, this energy can be slightly invoked by taking this facial posture. Various paintings of Zen teachers in China and Japan illustrate this set of facial traits and seem to be most commonly associated with the Rinzai sect, which puts emphasis on vigorous practices to bring about experiences of insight.

It is just these states of "feeling concentration" that the practitioner learns to appreciate and associate with "doing" Zen practice. The amount and intensity of this practice is directly related to one's ability to encounter such states. The collective practices of *sesshin* are especially important for the stimulation and support of such energies. In this context, when one moves far enough away from the practices and attitudes constitutive of everyday life, one begins to produce and sustain an alternative way of being.[14]

In asking about the theoretial term *hara* – whether members had any experience of *hara* in their sitting or practice and whether it was related to intensive sitting – I received the following responses.

No. That has been something I've had a real hard time grasping.... I never sat more than three-day *sesshin*s and I haven't done one of those in two years. So my way of coping with the pain of *sesshin* was to stop doing them (laughing). (no. 62)

Yes. [Someone] ... once related sitting to putting a kettle on to boil and if you get up every morning [and sit] that's keeping it on simmer.... And when you do *sesshin* it turns it up full force. I've noticed the boiling in *sesshin*.... I did a Mu

Mu *sesshin* one time . . . for a week. It was intense. We would all [make the sound] Mu at the top of our lungs for an hour. . . . Talk about *hara.* That was something that built my *hara* up to a boiling point. (no. 60)

I experience that more and more in my sitting. I have a sense of, ah, gravitating down to, you know, down there, down to where my hands are [in the sitting posture] over my stomach. In *sesshin* its very, very, very strong when I'm sitting. (no. 63)

As the *hara* comes together as an energy center, it is often experienced as strong energy flowing, as pleasantness, and as great stability and strength in the lower abdomen (Leggett, 1978, 78–79). One senior informant referred to these feelings as heat, as a squirrel running around in the lower abdomen. After periods of intensive practice, it is not emotions but feelings that are associated with an alert state of calmness and strength. The context of collective ritual practice seems essential for its cultivation for most people.

This chapter has examined ways in which the social organization of Zen ritual practice in *sesshin* facilitates an altered experience of self and reality. By limiting interaction to particular forms, I have argued that the *sesshin* occasion creates a context for self-mortification. Further, the *sesshin* setting organizes interaction in such a way as to reduce both self-consciousness and the level of attention usually devoted to managing social relations with others. Participating in *sesshin* also contributes to a learning of an altered mode and heightening of attention so that the normally unobserved operations of the mind become available. Not only the mind, but the body also becomes trained, more stable, more capable, and confident in doing the practices so that an experience of the self as witness to activities can occur. As Sudnow argues, intentionality is reduced in the process of doing the practice. Finally, the collective energies of group practice support individual commitment and involvement in the practice in such a way as to generate spiritual energies and a concomitant set of dispositions that I have called the Zen habitus.

CHAPTER IX

The Meanings of Zen Practice

Zen practice, like any phenomenon, depends for its meaning upon the particular presuppositions and practices used by particular individuals and groups to constitute it. Thus, for various people Zen can be silly, profound, esoteric, or ordinary. This chapter discusses three different meanings of Zen practice that are constituted by the intermingling of the assumptions and practices used by Zen practitioners on the one hand, and sociologists on the other. This typology of meanings bases itself in members' experience in the Zen setting but recognizes a variety of such experience. It also bases itself in sociological issues in the discussion of meaning but similarly recognizes a variety of positions on such issues.[1] Through this approach, I hope to contribute to the understanding of Zen practice, and similarly organized settings, as sets of relationships, assumptions, and practices that are constitutive of at least three forms of meaning – namely, conscious or subjective meaning, unconscious or objective meaning, and intuitive meaning.

Even though I want to argue that the process of becoming a member of a group using meditative practices involves more than mere resocialization and the learning of another way of being social, I readily admit that Zen can be seen as a meaning system. After all, despite all claims to the contrary ("if you meet the Buddha, kill him"), Zen is a sect of Buddhism that has, as one of the major world religions, a highly articulated theology. Most practitioners in the groups studied herein began Zen practice after finding its meaning appealing by reading about it. Tipton (1982) has argued that the close compatibility of meaningful themes in Zen and in the counterculture helps to account for the presence of former counterculture participants in Zen practice. People do Zen practice because they are acquainted at least theoretically with the notions of enlightenment and true Self, and because they think, believe, and feel that it is possible to accomplish a more desirable state of being. The ritual actions that are seen in the zendo (and many that occur outside as well) are meaningfully organized by the goal of enlightenment. One can speak of diverse elements in terms of their relationship to the "project" of enlightenment. Whether one sees the practices as a means to enlightenment, or as ways of expressing enlightenment already realized, is immaterial. To the extent that they occur as coherent discursive statements, both accounts are based in the ideas, symbolic universe, and cognitive presuppositions of Zen Buddhism.

But if we stop at this point in an analysis of Zen practice or other meditative traditions (or, as Collins, 1981, argues, even everyday life), the actual lived experience as well as unconscious influences on members' lives is drastically misconstrued. Continuing with the efforts made in earlier chapters, this section examines how the sense of shared meaning of often very private and idiosyncratic experiences encountered in Zen practice is produced in a context of ritual interaction. As seen in Chapter VIII, the experiences encountered by Zen practitioners, diverse as these are, are not produced simply by taking on a new set of beliefs and categories for making sense of the world. As I noted, few new interpretations are provided in place of old ones, no shaming takes place in the process of practice, new bodymind states are encountered and new energies stimulated, and the old self is shown to be illusory or flawed. Certainly some faith is necessary and some new symbolic meanings are learned, but emphasis is put immediately and recurrently on doing the practice. This emphasis on practice instead of knowing and talking about Zen is so strong in the groups studied that even persons like Alan Watts, who have written about Zen philosophically but neglect the notion of practice, are not taken very seriously by practitioners. As descriptions and analyses presented so far have insisted, Zen is in the doing of the practice, and this practice systematically slows, erodes, and makes visible the usual reality-building processes (personal and collective) used by all groups in everyday life.[2]

Because meditative practices facilitate this examination of normal reality-construction processes, they tend to create a distance from these mechanisms and do not quickly replace old forms and content with new categories. Some traditions do this more than others, of course. Because of its association with Taoism, Zen explicitly avoids the offering of alternative verbal accounts for making sense of things. The general framework of Buddhism is there, of course, but the Zen sect insists that important realization cannot be contained in words and discursive thought. In place of propositional knowledge, Zen says experiment for yourself. Do the practices and see what happens, what you experience. What happens can be rich and varied, depending on the individual.

Along these lines Brown (1977, 245) makes a most interesting point.

He notes that the form of meditation he analyzed has five levels of attainment, with each level having its own form of cognitive organization. Further, these stages are closely related to contemporary Western psychological theories of perception and emotion. The grossest level, for example, is tied to intellectual operations and the cognitive interpretation of emotions; the next deeper level is tied to perceptions (especially the theory of perception associated with Bruner and Neisser) and direct perception of autonomic activity. The more subtle levels concern finer and finer elements of information processing and autonomic activity.[3]

The typology of meaning in this chapter is somewhat similar. I argue that the subjective meaning of experience in Zen practice is a gross form of meaning production done largely by those practitioners who are least accomplished in the practice. It involves conscious activity in a way that constructionist theory suggests. The next level of meaning shared by some more advanced Zen practitioners is based in practice and experience that goes beyond these intellectual operations. Objective meaning production involves nonconscious, nonintentional processes that I will argue are based in the Zen habitus or in the dispositions to thinking (and nonthinking), feeling, and acting typical of Zen practitioners and based too in interactional rituals, as suggested by Collins (1981). This analysis could

Sesshin participants doing walking meditation (*kinhin*) on the grounds of the Los Angeles Center. Outside *kinhin* is used at times to invigorate a sleepy zendo.

be extended to other meditative groups having similarly deep structures, what Wilber refers to as religious groups on the causal level (1983, 30–1). This form of meaning is grounded in what I (after Wilber) have come to refer to as the bodymind to indicate a level of both body and mind training that produces in the practitioner an experience (among other things) of the separation of body and mind as an accomplishment of lower-level, reality-building cognitive processes. The third level of meaning addressed in this chapter, intuitive meaning, is really a form of nonmeaning by most definitions. It is not socially constructed (except in the ways indicated in the analysis throughout this work) or symbolically mediated. It resides in accomplishment in Zen practice (for us) that allows an awareness of the processes of reality construction (personal and collective) that can bring about an existential transformation in which (if one reads the teachers correctly) the problem of meaning ceases to exist. At this point I will stop, because to continue would take us beyond the furthest outposts of the sociological realm. I now turn to an elaboration of the processes of meaning production themselves.

Subjective (Conscious) Meaning

An earlier attempt (Chapter V) to deal sociologically with meaning in a Zen setting used a symbolic interactionist perspective. It followed rather closely the logic developed by Becker (1953) in showing a resemblance between a beginner to Zen practice and a person learning to use marijuana for pleasure. First, one must do it right if the "symptoms" are to be produced. If one does not do meditation properly, no consequences are produced, and one quits the practice. Second and, for the purposes here, most important, one must consciously connect the "symptoms" produced with having done sitting meditation. Otherwise, one stops doing it. I will provide a critique of just this point.

Another view of meaning construction that also puts emphasis on consciousness is that of the constructionist school. This work is primarily influenced by Schutz and Mead for understanding how the objectified world of symbolic objects comes to be experienced as subjectively meaningful. We already have an indication of Mead's theory of meaning from Becker's work. Meaning for Schutz on the other hand

is not a quality inherent in certain experiences emerging within our stream of consciousness but the result of an interpretation of a past experience looked at from the present now with a reflective attitude. As long as I live *in* my acts, directed toward the objects of these acts, the acts do not have any meaning. They become meaningful if I grasp them as well-circumscribed experiences of the past and, therefore, in retrospection. (Schutz, 1967, 210)

Meaning then is the result of the actor, alone or collectively, identifying and making sense of the objects and events of the world. This active doing can occur either before acting, as is the case with that class of human activity Schutz calls "action," or it can be done after acting, as is the case with what Schutz calls "conduct." For our purposes when practitioners do Zen practice with the goal of attaining "enlightenment" (whatever that might mean to them), they can be said to be engaging in social action in the full sense of the word "social." There is nothing esoteric about Zen practice conceived of in this way.[4]

The limits of the conscious construction of meaning in the Zen setting can be seen in Schutz's term "conduct." Not all of our activity is "action" that is conceived in advance. Much of our lives are filled with seemingly automatic or spontaneous activities – Schutz mentions habitual, traditional, and affectual forms – that nonetheless are subjectively meaningful in that they are retrospectively linked, by the individual, to conventional and normatively organized ways. Schutz does not consider spontaneous activity in detail, only its ability to be made meaningful by the actor. However, it is just this spontaneous activity that is most interesting for the purposes of our discussion. Regulated improvisation not only is a very large segment of our total activity, it also provides a topic for description and analysis that allows one to appreciate the limits of intention and consciousness in social activity in general.

Based on the analysis presented in Chapters VI, VII, and VIII, I believe that conscious and reflexive processes cannot be used to deal adequately with meaning much beyond the beginning stages of Zen practice. As argued in Chapter V, such conscious activity on the part of the beginner in Zen practice does indeed play a role in one's transformation into being a member of a Zen group. It was also seen, however, how the ritual organization of Zen practice attenuates the reflexive processes typical of everyday life. The zendo/*sesshin* setting eliminates the need for the negotiation/interpretation of meaning and makes this distance possible. Practicing in this setting alters the role of consciousness in social action as it is conceived of in both symbolic interactionism and in most other theories of social action. The selfing process is altered, as is the role of thinking as it occurs typically in everyday life. This contention is based on, and compatible with, members' experience. I now present an alternative notion of meaning and its production in a Zen setting.

Objective (Unconscious) Meaning

The definition of Zen practice developed in Chapters IV and VIII draws on the work of Bourdieu (1977) chiefly because he allows one to see this practice as a broad body-based training rather than merely cognitive, conscious learning and the reflexive construction of meaning. The work of Sudnow (1978), used extensively in Chapter VII, also reveals how the production of improvised conduct is closely tied to bodily training. Both Sudnow and Bourdieu, then, are concerned with regulated improvisation, the form of activity that I, after Bourdieu, call "objective meaning."

Regulated improvisation can be said to have objective meaning

because [one's] actions and works are the products of a *modus operandi* of which he is not the producer and has no conscious mastery, they contain an "objective intention" ... which always outruns his conscious intentions. The schemes of thought and action he has acquired are the basis for the *intentionless invention* of regulated improvisation. (Bourdieu, 1977, 79)

Unlike subjective meaning where one must either reflect on experience or anticipate it as part of a goal or purpose, objective meaning exists without conscious reflection. It is the result of the unconscious action of the habitus (subjective dispositions to forms of feeling, action, and thought typical of a group). Just as subjective and consciously derived meanings exist independently, they can also have this second dimension of meaning that is understandable to other group members despite there being no reason or intention on the part of the doer.

This objective meaning exists in the recognition by members of one's way of walking, playing, speaking, gesturing, and thinking as not only appropriate expressions of "our" way (as in "traditional" conduct), but even as especially clever and witty creations – improvisations – on such a way. A jazz musician's appreciation of another's musical improvisation is a particular example suggested by Sudnow. It is objective in the sense that both the doer and the hearer "recognize" its appropriateness but it is neither the product of an intention, as is usually assumed in social theory, nor the automatic reproduction of traditional forms. As will be shown, it is just such spontaneity or improvisation that becomes a key feature of action and experience in Zen practice. A somewhat different perspective of the same phenomenon can be found in the writings of Zen teachers. Yasutani (1973, 20) writes: "When the Way transforms a person's character and his way of life it does not break into his consciousness." Addressing such spontaneity is essential to a sociological understanding of Zen practice.

Besides spontaneity, the word "unconscious" appears in this discussion of objective meaning. Because the term unconscious normally is not used by sociologists, its meaning and value need to be established. Bourdieu helps us legitimate the use of this term, but Collins (1981) introduces it in a way that makes its value obvious. Collins is a conflict theorist and has interests that tend to emphasize the commonalities of humans and animals and the practical problems of maintaining legitimacy of social arrangements. Although I do not deny the importance and reality of such concerns, my interests are more in dealing with characteristics of humans that are shared with the "gods" and how these are accomplished in a socially organized ritual practice. There is no necessary contradiction.[5]

Basing his proposals on recent criticisms of rationalist and cognitive theories in sociology, Collins argues for an alternative notion of the social actor and social structure that is based on interaction ritual and emotional energies. He argues for a view of the social actor as one who does not think and calculate in terms usually imputed to the actor by social theorists, but rather as one who acts tacitly most of the time. People follow routines because they feel right in doing so, not because they know the norms, the situation, or the roles. Each actor participates in a set of conversational interaction rituals that provide the basis for group solidarity and personal identification.

Successful conversational interaction rituals are determined by participants being able to share a common cognitive reality (e.g., being able to talk in roughly the same way about the same things), and participants sustaining a common emotional tone or feelings of solidarity.

The fundamental mechanism [in making choices], then, is *not a conscious one*. Rather, consciousness, in the form of cultural resources, is a series of inputs into each situation.... It is possible, of course, for individuals sometimes to reflect consciously upon their social choices, perhaps even to become aware of their own cultural and emotional resources vis-à-vis those of their fellows. But the choices made, I would contend, would be the same as choices made without reflection. (Collins, 1981, 1005–1006; emphasis added)

A very similar conclusion is made by Fingarette (1963) about the process of decision or choice making. Even though his views are theoretically different from those of Collins, the view of the reflective subjectivity, usually held to be making the choice, is the same.

Things "come" to one who is profoundly, sensitively "open." Yet when the completed process is looked at by the observer and described in ordinary language, he says, correctly and idiomatically, that important decisions have been made. This language tends to support the myth of the crossroads "instant of choice." But we need not be confused by the misleading idiom, "make a decision"; we no more make a decision than it is made for us. Decisions take place when there is a genuine encounter between the person and his situation. (Fingarette, 1963, 56; emphasis dropped)

These elements of Collins' theory provide an alternative to common perspectives in sociology and are particularly suggestive for understanding features of the Zen setting.

Interestingly, although coming from different theoretical schools, both Collins and Sudnow agree on the diminished role of the "thinking self" in social conduct. In both their works, the roles of thinking, intending, and calculating are seen as less dominant, whereas the roles of the body and emotional (read "spiritual") energies are enhanced. This view of the social actor and social structure can be used to reveal how a shared sense of reality and objective meaning is produced in a Zen setting.

Objective Meaning Producing Processes in Zen Practice

Changes in the emotional basis of self and identity. People beginning Zen practice commonly have definite identities – that is, commitments about who they are, usually centered around the status categories of age, sex, class, and race. Even though our research indicates people who take up Zen practice are often disappointed with standard ways of life and their rewards, they are not so atypical that they are without the fetishes of appearance and ideology. Ways of dressing, of wearing one's hair, and so on form the basis of a sense of self that constitutes differences in the eyes of the person beginning Zen practice with a group. Participating in the rituals of Zen practice alters this perception of difference in a way that brings about a sense of likeness of kind among participants and a sense of shared experience. Although this might seem as simply a transfer of identity and loyalty from one set of group styles to another, in the meditative setting it turns on a somewhat different axis.

Participation in Zen practice – for example, bowing – can violate expectations that a person might have about what is dignified or proper. As sketched in Chapter VIII, engaging in this behavior can be mortifying to such a person, causing considerable emotional and cognitive distress. If one continues, however, to do the bowing (with the proper attitude), this practice eventually results in the diminution of these reactions, until only the bowing remains. The upsetting reactions are diminished in repeated practice, and that part of the person's identity that was distressed by such behavior is diminished as well. By not doing the work to maintain a sense of difference, the new practitioner comes to experience one's self in a new way. Still, it is important to see that a new identity as "Zen student" is not offered in place of the old one. Although some adopt such an identity, and perhaps all do to some degree, this is not the experience of more accomplished members nor is it, from the sociological viewpoint taken here, the consequence of the practices. As one experiences the new sense of self that just bows, for example, without thinking or emotion (positive or negative), one comes to realize that the others (who were previously considered quite different from one's self) also just bow with no thought or emotion. The resulting sense of likeness of kind is not a parochial sentiment, nor is it adequately captured by the term "feelings of solidarity." It is, however, a feeling and a sense of shared reality, one that is spoken of in rather different ways.[6]

Practitioners sense each other's commitment. Talk is eliminated in the zendo/*sesshin* setting, thus removing what many consider the single most important feature for shaping a common experience of reality. Using Durkheim's theory of ritual and Collins's (1975, 1981) recent work with it, other mechanisms are noticed whereby a sense of common reality is produced and sustained.

Individuals monitor others' attitudes toward social conditions, and hence toward the degree of support for routines, by feeling the amount of confidence and enthusiasm there is toward certain leaders and activities.... These energies are transmitted by contagion among members of a group. (Collins, 1981, 994)

When the sensed commitment to routines is high within a group, the realities – authority patterns, for example – associated with and supported by these routines are enhanced in the experience of participants. This applies directly to a Zen setting.

Upon beginning practice in the groups under study, I was struck by the sincerity and commitment of others. This attitude never waned over the course of a decade. Certainly there appeared to be some degree of difference in commitment in interviews with practitioners, but most were so highly committed that, in my view, spiritual leave-taking or holding back just was not available. I remember being surprised by a friend who attended a Tibetan retreat saying that he tended to associate and identify with the group of participants who were not pretentious. When I asked what he meant, he said that some participants were "obviously trying to give the impression of being more into it"; "holy" was the word he used. Although he might have made a similar observation at the setting considered here, I never heard any participant speak of practitioners in such terms. People did not pretend to be "into it" – either they were or were not. In fact, pretending is hardly possible, if pretending suggests faking the meditative state or some knowledge derived therefrom. Just as jazz improvisation cannot be faked except for the most naive and artless, accomplishment in meditative practice and the absence of such is manifest in one's actions. . For all practical purposes, there is little if any benefit in trying to pretend accomplishment, because there is no audience for such a performance in a zendo/*sesshin* setting. As noted, participants in *sesshin* keep their eyes down at all times, thus removing all but a few senior members responsible for monitoring the zendo and the teacher from even being able to be aware of a "performance." Further, how an individual might manifest accomplishment in any way that did not result in blending unnoticeably with the rest of the practitioners is unclear. Informal interaction outside the zendo/*sesshin* setting could provide an opportunity for role playing, although even here the saying, "Those who say do not know, and those who know do not say," tends to deflate much posturing of holiness.

The reality of collective support of individual practice can be seen in the groups studied in various ways. It is common to speak of "strong" sitters or participants in *sesshin* having a good influence on the group; included are those who can meet the demands of the *sesshin* and provide support, in chanting for example, for other, less ritually accomplished persons. A strong sitter is not necessarily a senior person, however. A beginner may give a brave effort to do the practice well. (Brave is not an inappropriate word at all in the *sesshin* context owing to the physical and mental demands made on the individual.) Further, instructions are regularly repeated as to how to hold the hands, how to bow, sit, walk, and so forth, so any deviance from these forms is obvious. Such deviance is extremely rare and usually that of the beginner.

The consequences of such commitment to Zen practice on the part of others is the emergence of a sense of reality shared by these others and support for one's efforts to experience such a reality. It is a very unusual feeling to be with people perceived to be like oneself who are actually committed to doing something, yet doing it without violating the deepest sense of value one holds about intellectual matters. One sees that the value of Zen practice is collectively endorsed. As Collins argues, this collective endorsement is not a reflexive process but rather is support in the form of energy that allows the practitioner to continue in the practice. One need not consciously (as Becker suggests) relate the practice to desired results. In fact, I find in interviewing practitioners that they grow increasingly uncertain as to why they attend *sesshin* or continue practicing. Some say "I don't know why" (this response is almost a popular form of expression among informants), others say "I can do no other." Because the practice effectively reduces reflexivity, any other account tends to be distrusted or disbelieved. Those who claim to be enlightened or to know what "Zen" is are viewed by members as clearly not knowing of what they speak. What Collins sees as an unconscious process of decision making on the basis of emotional energies, Buddhist (and other) theory sees as an attraction to enlightenment or to an intuited way of being that is already there but obscured by self processes.

Success in ritual activities. Collins (1981) argues that success in enacting membership rituals results in an increase in confidence in the actor. This well-taken point has an interesting twist in meditative settings. As seen in Chapter VIII, if one continues in the practice, some experience of ritual competence does develop, but it is such that the person who is ritually competent is different than the person who began the practice. The strategy of "figuring it out" and anticipating behavioral demands are inappropriate and counter-productive in this ritual setting. The speaking "I," the reflexive, verbal self cannot do the rituals of Zen practice competently.

The practitioner does come, then, to experience competence in ritual activities but it is despite, not due to, normal "selfing" operations. There is an increase in confidence certainly, but it is confidence and trust in a form of self or a way of being that is based in doing the practices repeatedly with others. The body becomes trained in the movements, the muscles and ligaments are lengthened and otherwise atuned to allow the accomplishment of the physical postures, so that comfort in sitting and grace in motion are possible and regular achievements. As this physical skill develops, the energies cultivated by meditative practices and the associated states of concentration, based in slowed reflexive activity and synchronized body processes, emerge. In this state ritual competence occurs, and eventually one comes to realize this consciously. Again, the theoretical terms of Zen, such as "true Self," are used to organize such experience consciously into indicators for one's career – as a Zen student, for example. This work, done to make sense of the ritual competence and more effective and confident spontaneity, however, is secondary to the actual state of being in which such appropriate behavior occurs. It is this unreflecting state that Zen training cultivates.

This awareness can occur not only in ritual activities but also in working periods associated with *sesshin* and ultimately in everyday life as well. One informant provides an experience from a *samu* period during *sesshin*.

I remember being assigned to replace some broken window panes. It was well along into a seven-day *sesshin*. I was using a hammer and chisel to remove the old putty and since the windows were ancient, it was rough going. At a certain point I turned back from fighting the putty and broken glass and the goal of finishing the work to the koan I had been working on for some years. Upon doing this I experienced a sudden and qualitative change in the flow of the work. Immediately and mysteriously the putty chipped off effortlessly and much faster than before. I have had this experience in a few other work projects as well. I only wish I could be in that space more often. (no. 26)

Being able to act effectively and appropriately – that is, to do what needs done – increases confidence and trust in one's self. The twist is that the self that is competent and trusted is not the willfully motivated, verbal, reflexive self we normally experience in everyday life. It is, on the contrary, the actively attentive, concentrated self that gradually emerges in the doing of Zen practice (and other similar sorts of practice).

Having this very practical, grounded experience of increased interactional competence further supports one in the activities of Zen practice whether consciously connected with the theoretical meaning of such practices or not. Typically, the practitioner does make the connection between personal experience and Zen theory, but the important connection is made not in the words but in the sensed availability of a desirable alternative way of being, feeling, and knowing.

Teacher–student interaction in private interviews. The student–teacher relationship is especially important for the production of a sense of shared meaning among practitioners. Because it is the only relationship during *sesshin* in which talk is allowed, it is often highly charged interaction and can have a strong impact on a student's efforts and understandings. In seeing the teacher in *dokusan,* a ritual form is followed that takes the student in and out of the interview room. The time spent between entering and leaving, however, is indefinite so that a student can use it to ask questions, make comments, or otherwise interact with the teacher. Its open and uncertain nature often makes students anxious. "What should I do?" Still, there are some regularities. If a student is working on a koan, the teacher will often say, "Show it to me," and expect the student to demonstrate his or her understanding of the koan. What "demonstrate" means is not particularly clear to the beginner or others for that matter. Despite working intensely on the koan, "How do you stop the sound of a temple bell?" for a couple of months, I was unable to understand it to my satisfaction until roshi helped me by talking briefly about sounds and where they originate and where they are perceived by me as being: "The birds chirping right now, where are they?" In this way I grasped the koan and was able to present it later in complete confidence to him. The step I had not taken was in grasping the "poetic" meaning of the koan as it applied to my experience. I was being too literal.

This experience in koan study was a turning point for me. I had learned that what I was already experiencing in sitting for some time was nothing else than that to which the teachings of Zen seemed to be pointing. While I still yearned for some profound experience, I became increasingly aware that the impact of sitting for extended lengths of time – that is, in *sesshin* – and over the course of several years seemed to have altered my perceptions in a way that my self, the reflexive, verbal, seemingly in-control, speaking "I," was not nearly as clearly defined as I had previously experienced it. Its boundaries had softened, at least when under the impact of intensive sitting during *sesshin.* At other times, it seemed as it had before. But a subtle change had occurred, and it was not only on the level of perception of sound, for example. I became convinced that I knew something, although I was not sure what it was. There was a conviction, a certainty that something was the case, yet I could not put it into words. (About this time, I also developed an interest in responding to sociological accounts of new religious settings that appeared to me to be mistaken.)

Talk by the teacher definitely helped me see my experience in a way that was "Zen" related, but more than the talk was involved. The sitting practice and other ritual practices produced the new perceptions to begin with. As Sudnow would say, the phenomenon was not merely a facet of an intending, speaking "I" and the reflexive process involved in language use. It also involved, perhaps primarily involved, the training of the body and mind in the doing of Zen practice.

Interaction with the teacher was particularly important, however, because before this interaction one's experience and knowledge is, no matter how powerful, still private, still unshared. On bringing such experience and knowledge to the teacher, one enters into a dialogue with a person who is seen to be advanced in the reality addressed.

Koan study might be seen in Collins's scheme as a long series of problematic interaction rituals where confidence can only be attained by seeing something significant in each koan. This constant reintroduction of uncertainty into the interaction ritual of *dokusan* reduces the chance of the student–teacher relationship becoming merely a mundane one. Having success in past interactional rituals is not enough. The present koan is what is being tested, and it alone is relevant. Of course, if the student really sees – that is, if one has a significant insight and profound experience – then, teachers say, koans become clear in one flash, and one's understanding can be demonstrated confidently.

Confidence flows from a spontaneous response to the teacher's request for a demonstration of the koan. As many have noted from Zen and other contexts, it is only in being able to do this confidently and spontaneously to some degree that it is satisfactory to self. It is also interesting that without constant practice one tends to forget insights and meanings previously encountered so that one's confidence erodes.

I believe in a way similar but not limited to that of Collins, that practicing meditative rituals tends to produce an experience of self that is decidedly different. It is a nonverbal, noncalculating self rooted in an altered attitude of attention to life that is both competent and confident in action. The performer as intending subjectivity is eliminated in the sense that the performer is trying to do officially prescribed activities, or some idiosyncratic version thereof, that are meant to demonstrate one's particular identity. One disappears in the doing of the prescribed activity, eliminating self-consciousness (defined by Fingarette [1963, 312] as intrapsychic conflict and anxiety but visible sociologically in terms of reduced reflexivity activities). When appropriate behavior can be done spontaneously and without self-consciousnes, one notices this conduct

A monk doing a full bow. The characteristic gesture of raising the hands above the head is said to symbolize elevating the Buddha or true Self above the empirical self.

and experiences self in a different fashion than previously. This phenomenon is not to be understood entirely as habitus (dispositions to thinking, acting, and feeling) or as an unconscious but still socially mediated process of conduct, as described by Collins – that is, it is not to be seen as below the conscious faculty for meaning production. On the contrary, I see this phenomenon as a neglected human capability that is pursued by others under a variety of rubrics: the "existential self" (Kotarba & Fontana, 1984; Tiryakian, 1968) the "transpersonal" level of consciousness (Wilber, 1983); the symbolic self (Natanson, 1970); or that part of the social self called the "I" (Mead, 1934) in contrast to the "Me" that is more clearly reflexive and limited to, and by, the more mundane processes of everyday life. Of course, in the Zen setting this capability is seen by members as being directly related to the Buddhist concept of "true Self."

Objective meaning is interesting for two reasons. First, as it manifests in an individual's behavior, both self and others recognize objective meaning as appropriate activity in a particular situation. It has (often) a quality of spontaneity and directness that is surprising. One does not intend it, nor is it habitual or traditionally prescribed in its form. It is an improvised form that expresses itself through an individual but is more than what the individual intends. Second, this process allows the practitioner to see a new capability of action and a new form of self that was not recognized previously in the modality of meaning where one was constantly either planning action or retrospectively finding it meaningful because it was habitual or traditional in form. This new sense of self (and the competence and confidence associated with it) contributes to the disidentification with the self with which one entered the practice and contributes to a sense of accomplishment in the Zen way. This brings us to the third form of meaning, namely, intuitive meaning.

Intuitive (Fundamental) Meaning

Wilber writes, very simply, that intuitive meaning involves finding that

the very processes of life itself generate joy. Meaning is found, not in actions or possessions, but in the inner radiant currents of your own being, and in the *release and relationship* of these currents to the world, to friends, to humanity at large, and to infinity itself. (1979, 119–20)

He has an elaborate theory of the transpersonal that expands upon such a simple statement, which we need not consider here. What is most relevant for our purposes is his claim that "spiritual knowledge itself is *not* symbolic; it involves direct, nonmediated, trans-symbolic intuition of and identity with spirit" (Wilber, 1983, 133). Thus, this sort of meaning involves a knowing that allegedly escapes from the determinism of other forms of human endeavor. This claim is so audacious as to make those who are not entirely sympathetic reject any further discussion of the topic.

When Wilber makes such a claim, however, he does not mean that this form of meaning knowledge exists in a vacuum. On the contrary, I have previously taken Wilber's advice to study the psychosocial relationships constitutive of this form of meaning and have argued that we must qualify considerably the usual relationships that are held to obtain between a particular group's environmental structures, reality production processes, and their cultural productions, which make these productions mere forms of "local knowledge."[7] Engaging in Zen practice (in this case) does more than just horizontally translate the practitioner's previous local knowledge into a Zen form of local knowledge. (It can of course do so, as the two previously discussed forms of meaning admit.) Because participation in meditative practice tends to slow the automaticity of personal (Deikman, 1966) and collective reality-building processes, the accomplished practitioner comes to look at rather than just through forms previously taken for granted (Brown, 1977; Wilber, 1977, 198–346). Hence, in the process of practice, as one learns to do conscious meaning construction on one's experience, and as one learns to do the prescribed activities of Zen practice more competently and confidently, thereby encountering objective meaning, there is also developing an increasing ability to enter into an altered state of consciousness. This state (or states) is sometimes referred to as the various stages of samadhi or levels of concentration. The existence of such states of consciousness and their relationship to accomplishment in meditative practices is widely accepted, although relatively neglected as a topic of study.

An effort that attempts the study of the levels of consciousness related to meditation reports that in the classic literature on meditation

the language used is linked to the state or level of consciousness of the individual, and the meaning of the term can only be understood by the meditator who has reached a certain level of advancement in his experiences arising in meditation. Otherwise, the language appears "nonsensical" and has no meaning for them. Hence, the language is largely specific to meditation populations and to particular levels reflective of the meditator's degree of advancement. (Maliszewski et al., 1981, 15)

Maliszewski and colleagues cite Tart's (1975) theory of state-specific communication to suggest that communication in one particular state of consciousness is different from communication in another. One conclusion Tart makes is that it might be impossible for persons who have not experienced meditative states, for example, to understand what is happening within such states. Because this is quite likely true, I will limit myself to examining those forms and features of relationships and communication in the Zen setting that are constitutive of this intuitive meaning. By doing so, I want to make clear how the social organization of Zen practice contributes to an agreement on such meaning by testing and providing feedback to practitioners that either supports or negates particular "demonstrations" of that meaning (Wilber, 1983). In other words, the language and state of consciousness in which the present communication occurs does not hope to grasp intuitive meaning. It merely allows us to understand how members, particularly advanced members in Zen settings, produce an agreement on intuitive meaning using (among other "things") socially organized practices.

These techniques are not essential for accessing this level of reality, however, as is suggested by Wilber's comment about the historical roots of meditative practices in Zen as techniques for facilitating insight.

The Supreme Vehicle of Ch'an (Zen) Buddhism began as a "direct pointing to Mind" and a "seeing into one's Self-Nature," without apparently emphasizing any spiritual means or exercises, such as concentration or meditation.... Few people, however, were awake and aware enough to see *this* directly, and so over the centuries that Ch'an grew and developed in China,... it began to create ingenious *upaya* [skillful means] to help persons of all mentalities awaken to Mind, such as the shouting of Ma-tsu, Lin Chi, and Yun-men, the striking of Ma-tsu and Te-shan, the *koan (hua tou)* of Yuan-wu and Ta-hui, and the "silent Illumination" associated with Tien-tung. (1977, 322)

The original emphasis on intuitive insight and meaning in the Zen tradition is clear. In its most subtle form, then, no particular techniques are necessary either to facilitate the insight or express it.

The description and analysis in this work, however, has dealt with the details of the present organization of Zen practice in two groups in the United States. A rather wide variety of elements of these settings, not only those mentioned by Wilber, are taken as important features of Zen practice that can have a decided impact on the practitioner's consciousness and behavior. When intuitive meaning is examined to learn how it is constituted by the social organization of Zen practice, literally all of the descriptions and analyses presented in this and other chapters are relevant. As noted previously, Zen practice attentuates old reality building practices, facilitates a new experience of the bodymind, and uses emotional sources of support for practice and for the embodying of new ways of being.

The basis of intuitive meaning is an experience that has various names, such as enlightenment, *kensho, satori,* peak experience, and mystical experience. Not only are these experiences important, but even less striking or profound experiences that occur during meditative practice are related to intuitive meaning. Some of these experiences have been discussed in earlier chapters. They include increased relaxation, including deeper, slower breathing; slowing of excessive mental activity; an ability to focus more clearly on the details of consciousness and the processes of reality construction; both an increased awareness of the body and a reduction of sensation arising in the body; a cultivation of spiritual energies; and a moderation of excessive emotionality. Intuitive meaning has to do with feelings of joy but also with freshness, immediacy, and an absence of jadedness, ambivalence, revulsion, or boredom. A very simple case of intuitive meaning can be illustrated in the following way.

Both Weber and Schutz find meaning in the process of relating means to ends or, said differently, in the coherence that an overall goal or project gives to the elements that constitute it. Each increment in an ongoing project is seen to gain its meaning from its incorporation into the broader project. Thus, what is rational in a particular context depends on the proper selection of the appropriate means to attain a particular end. Intuitive meaning, on the other hand, arises in a different, yet related manner.

While writing this, the need arises for a special pen. The flow of the writing is broken off, and I turn to the drawer in my desk where the pen supposedly is. The drawer is crowded, however, and the pen is not immediately available. A feeling of blockage begins to arise in me as the goal-oriented momentum of the writing project pulls my attention back to the writing process and away from the search for the pen. But the pen is needed to continue the project, so a conflict exists. Frustration, expressing itself as the tightening of muscles in the throat, face, and abdomen, increases as the mind and body engaged in the writing project is forced to slow down because of the unavailability of the needed pen.

Then, noticing this tightening of the muscles because of the interrupted project, I switch to a fresh experience of just looking for the pen. Hands are moving in the drawer and the eyes are searching, unhurried, with enjoyment in just this act. This enjoyment of just this looking for the pen is made possible by the meditative practices and is grounded in the increased attention to the bodymind and its fluctuating forms. Without continued practice, the frustration is not noticed until much later and not interrupted, with the result that the blockage of the project is the main experience rather than the simple act of looking for the pen. Perhaps it is not even appropriate to call this intuitive meaning, but it is clearly not action whose meaning (subjective) is organized by a project – in fact, it is just the opposite. It is satisfying to the extent that the project is forgotten; nor is what we address to be grasped as objective meaning beyond the intention of the actor. Instead it is constituted as fundamentally meaningful to the degree that it is just this act, just now, completely fresh and immediate. It is not located reflexively in any past or future, yet this act is even more effective because it is not interferred with by the tightening of the bodymind around the interruption of the project of writing. I give the looking for the pen my full attention and, on finding it, return to the writing. There certainly is nothing very esoteric about this action. In fact, it is just ordinary mind aware of itself, and more free, less conditioned, because of it. The key is the grounding of this capability in an ongoing, disciplined practice.

I am concerned with examining the social processes whereby members go about producing an agreement on the existence of such insight or understanding on the part of particular individuals in particular situations. Such testing is possible because, Wilber argues

spiritual knowledge, *like all other forms of valid cognitive knowledge,* is experimental, repeatable, and publicly verifiable, because, like all other valid modes, it consists in three strands: 1. *Injunction:* always of the form, "If you want to know this, do this." 2. *Apprehension:* a cognitive apprehension—illumination of the "object domain" addressed by the injunction. 3. *Communal Confirmation:* a checking of results with others who have adequately completed the injunctive and illuminative strands. (1983, 133)

Just as any ritual can be an occasion for individual practice, it can also be taken as an occasion for testing of an individual on the part of a teacher. Two particular rituals, *dokusan* (already examined in some detail) and *shosan* (dharma combat), include testing of the student's understanding as main features of their organization. Both make clear the importance of testing and show how teachers and senior members go about seeing accomplishment in Zen training manifested in behavior of particular individuals.

There seem to be behavioral indicators of accomplishment in Zen practice that allow senior members of this practice (as well as senior members in similar meditative traditions) to recognize approximate levels of understanding and accomplishment in others. One teacher said:

I can tell right away where a person is in their practice by the way they bow on the way into interview. If they do a full bow very quickly and hop right up, it provides me with certain information about them. How a person bows varies with their *samadhi*. The ability to give oneself to the present moment is a measure of accomplishment. (Field notes, 7 April 1984)

According to another teacher:

The thoughts and words are about reality.... It's like trying to eat a menu in a restaurant rather than the food. Not very satisfying. So that's why teachers are always saying to the students "I don't want to hear your ideas, I don't want to hear your concepts, I don't want to hear your words. Show it to me! – with your whole body, with your whole mind." That's the point of Zen practice. It's not a discussion about who I am, it's being who I am. It's the taste, the touch, the smell, the sound of who I am.[8]

Not just teachers but members also speak of being able to tell that someone was "getting into it," "sitting well," and so on. The trained eye can see accomplishment in Zen training that goes beyond mere ritual competence. It seems that the bodymind reflects the state of one's being. Because relaxation and concentration are so central to meditative practices, body postures and movements that are not harmonious with such states stand out as indicators of poor practice and vice versa. Nervousness, shallow breathing, and rapid eye movements are some of the grosser indicators.

The details of such knowledge are not very well known to members, however, perhaps because so much of their attention is focused inward on their individual practice. Only teachers really have the opportunity to notice the nuances in behavior in the zendo and correlate it with knowledge of an individual's accomplishment. In addition to obvious cues, there are those that can be used in evaluating a person and a situation but cannot be specified in terms of sense data. One teacher said in this context, "We know many things about people and a person without being able to say just how it is we know it." Fingarette offers similar thoughts.

I would suggest that a primary reliable clue to profundity of insight ... is the degree of personal autonomy connected with that insight. To what extent does the person not only talk the game but actually behave with spontaneity and yet with purpose? Does he show sensitivity to facts and claims along with an absence of bondage to them? ... Further, when all is said and done, the practical test is not in *a priori* claims or philosophical name-throwing, but in practice – sustained, serious, constantly critical, and sensitive practice. (1963, 61–2)

This latter comment by Fingarette suggests a holistic basis for evaluating accomplishment of practitioners. Not just particular behaviors or particular verbal forms are evaluated, but the qualities of attention, spontaneity, and subtlety are also noticed. Enthusiasm is not enough. One participant in *shosan* (dharma combat) who claimed to have recently had an important experience *(kensho)* of insight and who kept saying, "Isn't it wonderful, Isn't it wonderful," was rather sharply dismissed by the senior monk with the comment, "No. You stink." This response did not deny the experience but simply reminded this participant, as well as others attending the ritual, that it is an error according to Zen teachings "to attach to" experiences. It was an error that was negatively sanctioned in

Oryoki (bowls) on shelves awaiting use by *sesshin* participants. Notice the unique knot that ties each set of bowls, utensils, and linens into a single, tight unit.

a strong and public fashion. Of course, not everyone is addressed so strongly, even in *shosan*. The general rule is, the stronger and more confident the student, the stronger the teacher can be in providing the necessary feedback. Often it is difficult to find much more than gentle encouragement for most students in the *shosan* ritual.

Intuitive meaning then is not constituted linguistically or via a project reflexively. It is not produced mechanistically or habitually, although it can be seen to be linked to a set of dispositions formed in Zen practice. Instead, intuitive meaning is a returning to the present and finding it fresh by allowing meaning to emerge from life itself. Merleau-Ponty was on common ground when he wrote:

In the silence of primary consciousness can be seen appearing not only what words mean, but also what things mean: the core of primary meaning round which the acts of meaning and expression take shape. (1962, xv)

CHAPTER X

Summary and Conclusions

The phenomenon examined in this study has been the experience of practitioners in two Southern California Zen groups. The writer has been a member of these groups for some ten years and at a certain point felt a need to deal with this experience in terms of sociology. More specifically, this need developed about the time of the Jonestown incident, when accounts in the media of religious, especially cultic, settings were not adequately informed of the differences between Jonestownlike and, say, Zenlike settings. Early efforts to articulate these differences between what many in the press were calling "cults" and treating pejoratively and my own experience led me to begin reading in the sociology of religion. This literature seemed limited in that much of it was written by authors who were not associated with the kinds of religious settings that I was interested in exploring. The result was an oversocializing of the phenomenon that may have been convincing to some sociologists but was inadequate in meeting a member's test of validity. Of the various perspectives represented, those of the interactionists were the most palatable to me, with their emphasis, for example, on how an individual goes about participating in a religious conversion; they avoided the more typical question of why the participant was passively, more or less determined by circumstances, to convert. Further, many of these sociologists who were prone to examine religious experience of the sort that interested me were not aware of some striking differences between various religious settings and between some religious settings and secular settings. They recommended treating what goes on in religious conversion simply as another case of resocialization – in a word, as nothing special.

In trying to apply symbolic interactionism, what I considered the best of these approaches, to the Zen setting, I found (as discussed in Chapter V) that it had very definite limits. Its emphasis on conscious processes in learning makes it most appropriate for studying the beginning stages of involvement in Zen practice, where social learning of a sort held to be common in everyday life and settings occurs. However, this approach deals adequately with neither the subconscious physiological impact of meditative practices, measured as reduced mental and physical anxiety for example, nor the increased concentration and slowing of reflexive consciousness produced therein.

Other interactionists, roughly termed cognitive constructionists, provide an alternative to symbolic interactionism by the study of cognitive presuppositions and practices in the production of social phenomena. Although there is a wide range of sociologists who work within this general realm, those who take reality production in religious settings seriously are clearly the most relevant. They tend to notice special features of reality or meaning in settings that cultivate mystical experience. This general view of shareable experience being the result of shared reality-production processes has been used throughout the remainder of this study, but with some necessary modifications to take into account unique features of meditative settings. As a result of these modifications – supplemented with the noncognitive, body-centered theories of reality construction – a rather different notion of the social actor and reality construction has emerged.

Meditative settings cannot be treated as "nothing special." If one does, the special features of such settings and the experience of members therein are obviously missed. Doing meditation tends to produce an increased ability to concentrate among practitioners that follows from the practice of looking at, not just through, the normal reality-producing mechanisms. Along with this process, there is a decided reduction in reflexive thought and language use generally recognized to be *the* vehicle of reality production. Finally, meditative practice can result in a deconditioning of deep-rooted personal habits of perception and action. Consequently, an account of reality production in meditative settings (like Zen) needs to be generated.

This study has attempted to generate such an account by drawing on social theorists whose work takes seriously the concept of humans as embodied beings. Rather than ignoring the body and focusing primarily on mental operations, this account of meditation in a Zen setting deals explicitly with bodily energies and their relationship to social organization. Because meditation involves a slowing of discursive mental processes, the role of the body in the reality produced in meditative settings is set in relief and found to be central. It is not taken simply as an opposite to the one-sided view of social actors as thinking, knowing, believing beings, however. Rather, both the body and mind have been viewed as key to the mode of experience produced in meditative settings, and the concept of bodymind was used to suggest this nondualistic relationship.

The work of Sudnow was used as an exemplar to illustrate the development of this notion of bodymind in the process of Zen meditation. It has allowed an illustration of the process whereby regulated improvisation (defined as conduct that is perceived by others as appropriate, even exemplary, yet not planned in advance) and an alternative awareness of self is accomplished in Zen meditation. It has provided an example of the reduced role of the speaking I, of intentionality. Of course, Sudnow means this argument to apply to much of activity in everyday life, which could profitably be seen as conduct, that is, as regulated improvisation. If language use in the form of talk is seen in this way, then social theories that use language and talk as the main mechanism of shared reality construction will need to modify their accounts of the social actor and rationality. Zen meditation provides a case for the application of Sudnow's general point, and to this degree the seeming specialness of meditative settings vis-à-vis constructionist theory becomes much less special. Sudnow's highly innovative view of regulated improvisation allows the production of a sociological account of experience in Zen meditation, and the experience of meditators provides a grounding for Sudnow's theory.

Whereas Sudnow's work has helped produce a sociological account of sitting meditation, the concepts of Bourdieu were used to view Zen practice in general. He provided a statement of the importance of practice within a particular environment and the production of subjective dispositions shared by a group of practitioners. Here, too, cognitive capabilities are not ignored but rather located in a broader theoretical context where the body is taken seriously. The Zen retreat *(sesshin)* was taken as an example of a Zen environment, or of structures (in Bourdieu's sense), in which practice occurs and an altered form of subjectively shared dispositions to thinking, feeling, and acting develops. Because the *sesshin* setting is a highly organized ritual practice, the work of Goffman, Durkheim, and Collins has been used to examine the role of ritual interaction in the production and alteration of self and society and to provide details of how Zen ritual practice alters reality-building processes. Just as was the case with using Sudnow's ideas to see Zen meditation, using the theories of Bourdieu, Collins, Durkheim, and Goffman to view Zen ritual practice reduces the seeming specialness of this practice. Again much of what appears to be esoteric is constituted by not taking social influences on the body and the bodymind sufficiently into account. Once it is accepted that not all settings are the same, that not all practitioners or people in general are in the same "space," and that meditative practices are a special case of features of social settings that need to be more adequately dealt with theoretically and descriptively, then much of the specialness of reality construction in the Zen setting disappears. Sociology has only just begun to take these complex points seriously.

How then is Zen to be viewed? What is "Zen"? To symbolic interactionists, Zen is a social phenomenon learned in a group context using conscious processes of symbolic reality construction. To theorists like Collins, Zen is a reality produced by practitioners doing particular ritual practices in a particular environment whereby particular bodily energies are produced, synchronized, and shared via emotional contagion. As such, it is a reality produced in a way very different from most received theories of social action and reality construction and to a degree deserving of the title "transcultural." To others, such as Wilber, the reality shared by Zen practitioners is certainly constituted in particular psychosocial relationships, but it is ultimately symbolically unmediated, transpersonal, and open-ended to the experience of the divine.

The present study has tried to specify some of the special features of one of the settings that claim to provide access to or expression for these transpersonal levels of consciousness. It has identified socially organized practices that contribute to the attenuation of habitual and commonsensical reality-construction processes and that facilitate an alternative experience of reality. It is an effort to develop a theoretical language that allows for the fact of members' experience in meditative settings and for the possibility of its construction in a socially organized fashion. If we are to be true to reality as it is encountered by members (which is not to say to "go native" in the worst sense of the word), then this effort must be undertaken. No assumptions about what will be found need be made, but such a project clearly recognizes the limits of treating humans as, at best, creatures whose highest achievements are the result of chiefly mental ruminations. Beyond such a rationalistic model of human beings lies another that has been called the transpersonal or the transcultural. This model suggests possibilities for developing and understanding our lives together that go well beyond the assumptions and perspectives presently dominating social theory.

Appendix

Table 1. *Characteristics of Zen Center Members Participating in Surveys*

	Sample		
Social Characteristics	1980 ($N = 47$)	1980 ($N = 14$)	1984 ($N = 14$)
1. Marital Status			
Single	16	6	8
Married	15	4	4
Divorced	12	2	2
Other	4	2	0
2. Religion of Family of Origin			
Protestant	24	9	7
Catholic	8	2	6
Jewish	11	3	1
Other	4	0	0
3. Employment			
Full-time	33	6	9
Part-time	3	4	5
Unemployed	11	4	0
4. Education			
Years completed			
≤ 12	3	0	0
≤ 16	19	5	5
> 16	25	9	9
5. Degrees			
None	12	2	4
B.A. or B.S.	18	5	1
M.A. or M.S.	9	5	9
Ph.D.	8	2	0

Table 1 (*cont.*)

Social Characteristics	Sample		
	1980 (N = 47)	1980 (N = 14)	1984 (N = 14)
6. Presently Attending School			
Yes	2	3	3
No	45	11	11
7. Field of Study or Major			
Humanities	12	6	1
Sciences	12	5	4
Social sciences	9	2	4
Arts	3	0	2
Religious studies	2	1	0
Other	2	0	2
None	7	0	1
8. Class of Family of Origin			
Lower	2	0	3
Middle	44	14	11
Upper	1	0	0
9. Influenced by the Counterculture			
Yes	28	9	8
No	16	2	4
Perhaps	3	3	2
10. Previous Drug Use			
Marijuana			
Yes	40	10	13
No	7	4	1
Psychedelics			
Yes	27	7	7
No	20	7	7
11. Political Classification			
Apolitical	4	3	–
Radical	6	4	–
Liberal	7	3	–
Moderate	3	1	–
Conservative	1	0	–
Other	26	3	–
12. Experience in Other New Religious, Therapeutic, or Martial Arts Setting			
0–1 settings	15	2	11
2 settings	11	3	3
3 or more	14	7	0
Only est	7	2	0

Table 2. *Sex of Zen Center Members (selected populations and samples)*

Practitioners	Male	Female	Total
All practicing members (except residents) at Los Angeles Center 1980	78	68	146
1980 sample	27	20	47
All members at San Diego Center 1984	41	28	69
New member sample 1980	8	6	14
New member sample 1984	11	3	14

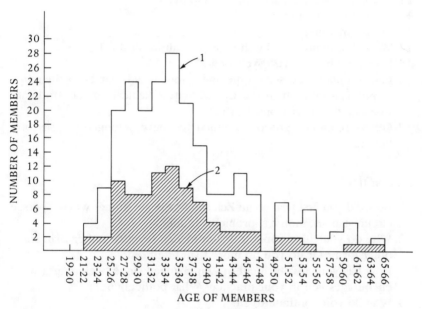

Figure 1. Age of Practitioners, Los Angeles Center 1980: (1) residents and practicing members, (2) residents only (shaded).

Questionnaire

Section I

1. Code number of interview
2. Age?
3. Sex?
4. Religious background of family and one's religious career?
5. Occupation of head of household when in high school?
6. Present marital status?
7. Years of education completed?
8. Presently attending school?
9. Field of study or major?
10. Degrees?
11. Working full-time, part-time, unemployed?
12. Present occupation?
13. Annual income?
14. Were you influenced by the counterculture of the 1960s?
15. Ever used marijuana? Psychedelics?
16. Can you place yourself on the line below, which stands for the range of political opinion in the United States? Radical Liberal Moderate Conservative Very Conservative
17. Other "religious" groups to which you have belonged or presently belong?

Section II

1. How did you first hear about Zen and first begin sitting? When? (pursue circumstances, motives, problems in life?)
2. Why do you think you are drawn to Zen practice rather than some other form? Or do you do more than one form?
3. How has your involvement in Zen changed since beginning? (What encourages you in your practice? What bothers you?)
4. Why do you continue to sit?
5. How did you come to be a student of your present teacher?
6. How did you come to be more involved in the practice here?
7. What aspects of the practice do you enjoy the most? The least? (e.g., service and other ceremonies?)
8. What do you like most about living at the Center, or practicing at the Center?
9. What are the people who practice Zen like? Are those in Los Angeles different from those in San Diego, for example? Are they different from people in general?

10. What were your original perceptions of Zen practitioners or the Center, and how have they changed over time?
11. Would you say you have many or few contacts with other members of the sangha? (i.e., place yourself in the community of practitioners.)
12. How do you think the Center looks to people who have no interest in Zen and no information about it? (e.g., people living around the Center?)
13. What do you think the consequences of the practice are? How might it change American society?

The 1984 interviews were based on this same set of questions with some additions made to reflect new interests and deletions of nonproductive material. The question on politics was dropped in 1984 and a specific question on acquaintanceship with the theoretical meaning and experience of the term *hara* was added.

All but a few interviews were tape-recorded. The average time of each interview was about forty-five minutes with some going considerably longer.

The questions in Section II deal with issues in the study of conversion and commitment processes in sociology and are similar to those asked by Tipton (1982), although arrived at independently. For various reasons, these questions did not produce information that was particularly helpful in understanding the subtlety of these processes in the groups studied. We understand this to be an artifact of the particular sort of reality shared in Zen groups, namely, that members resist explicit formalization of their experience in discursive terms.

Notes

I. A Sociological View of Zen

1   See Bush & Simmons (1981) and Gecas (1981) for a discussion of the social psychological literature on socialization.
2   See Robinson & Johnson (1982) for a discussion of the place of Zen in the broader Buddhist context.

II. A Profile of Zen Membership and Formal Organization in Southern California

1   Some developments in Zen communities that occurred a few years ago in the United States have raised questions about these settings. Open breaks and even near disintegration have occurred in several communities. For those acquainted with Zen groups in this country, such occurrences were a surprise if not a shock. These events are a major turning point in the development of Zen in the United States. So far, attention has been focused largely on the teachers – e.g., a collection of articles and notes in the *Co-evolution Quarterly,* Winter 1983, examining the role of the teacher. Informal discussions among practitioners often consider this topic as well. A more considered account of these events is still needed.
2   For an account of the arrival of Zen in the United States, see Fields (1981).
3   See Jacobs (1984) for a discussion of the sexual exploitation of females in various religious groups.
4   The following description was written in 1984 and does not reflect important changes since that time.

III. The Zen Teacher

1   Private correspondence, Jikan, 13 June 1983.
2   It is important to notice that the above first-person account is not intended to be autobiographical but rather to provide evidence of a typical member's experience in Zen practice.

IV. What is Zen?

1   I am not concerned with mystical experience per se in this account of Zen practice. This all too facile term does not do justice to the experiences of the groups studied and tends to ignore the less spectacular experiences of everyday practice. I am interested in states of increased concentration *(samadhi)* rather than mystical experiences, although they are related. I am in no position to speak of mystical experience personally (as tied to Zen practice) and have heard few accounts of such from my informants.

2   There appear to be two main kinds of meditation. In the simplest sense, concentrative forms involve a limiting of attention to a particular item of awareness, such as counting one's breath or focusing on the koan: "A monk in all seriousness asked Joshu: "Has a dog Buddha nature or not?" Joshu retorted, 'Mu!' " Brown (1977) provides an excellent discussion of this sort of meditation. The mindfulness form of meditation, on the other hand, involves watching the mind in operation without any attempt to control or limit its flow. Often the practitioner is instructed to just notice what happens and to label it – for example, thinking, feeling, smelling, or daydreaming. For excellent discussion of this process of "mindfulness" meditation, see King (1980) and Thera (1969).

3   Application forms for participation in Zen retreats *(sesshin),* for example, ask questions about the applicant's emotional stability and recent involvement in therapy.

4   The difference between what Yasutani calls the lesser and the greater Buddhist ways goes beyond mere forms of practice, however. While not developed in the present study, a broader (extracultic) supporting culture that cognitively roots religious experience in everyday life by making it expected and normal is instrumental in the development of a more integrated experience of Buddhism. See Damrell's (1977, 231–2) discussion of this point.

5   See Balch (1980) and Wilson (1984) on how this occurs in other groups.

6   See Park (1983) for a discussion of the role of faith in enlightenment.

7   From a mimeographed copy of a dharma talk by Maezumi-roshi in the Zen Center Los Angeles Newsletter, July 1982.

8   Yasutani lists this experience of awakening as the second goal of *zazen,* and it is seen as directly related to the first goal – namely, the development of the ability to observe the mind in operation and to still the waves of everyday consciousness. This is not the final stage of practice in either Wilber's scheme or in Zen. The final goal of Zen for Yasutani is the actualization of this way – that is, using the insights and knowledge glimpsed in *kensho* – in daily life.

9   The limitations of treating meditation or any other ritual form as a technique, as a way of accomplishing something, need be made explicit. Various sayings by Zen teachers demand this: "There is no such thing as Zen." "We sit because we are enlightened, not to become enlightened." "There is nothing one can do, except to do nothing."

D.T. Suzuki makes this same point more discursively in his discussion of Japanese spirituality (1972). Zen is usually recognized as taking root in Japan around the thirteenth century, but Suzuki notes that what was actually introduced from China at that time was Zen ritual, symbols, and systems. These, he argues, necessarily follow the insight of spiritual experience, not precede it. Bringing the experience to a people in the form of symbols and rituals is not possible. They must be ready for them before they can truly use them. Otherwise, he argues, they become mere formalisms in the observance of the ways of a religion.

By noting this now, I hope to avoid the criticism of being too simple and of misleading the reader in my description of Zen practice. Certainly there are individuals, and even whole groups, who are less genuinely involved than others. Wilber (1983) makes a point of identifying the degree to which a particular group is genuinely involved in the practice. The groups studied herein have a wide range of individual accomplishment but the cores of the groups themselves, changing as they are, are very well accomplished in the practices of Zen. Zen practice is for them no mere formalism.

V. Meditation as a Social Phenomenon: I

1 With a few changes, the material presented in this chapter appeared previously in Preston (1981).
2 For example, see the two excellent articles by Gordon (1984) and Wilson (1984).
3 Taken from a mimeographed copy of a talk, "Zazen and Christianity," by Koun Yamoda-roshi given in Kamakura, Japan, in 1975.
4 The writings of teachers who warn against "spiritual materialism" are evidence of this practice of clinging to experiences (Trungpa, 1973).

VI. Meditation as a Social Phenomenon: II

1 Wilson (1984) has begun to deal with this inadequacy by arguing a difference between resocialization and deconditioning in the context of a particular type of religious setting. This point is developed later in this discussion.
2 See, for example, Damrell (1977), who describes in a straightforward fashion a Vedanta group in California that uses what he calls a phenomenological perspective.
3 See Tipton (1982) for a discussion of meaning in a Zen setting that is considerably different from the one presented here.
4 Nearly half of all students encountered in sociology of religion classes claim to be already familiar with it, having encountered similar experience (they suppose) in a wide range of activities such as the martial arts, jogging, periods of religious retreat, hiking, drugs, therapy, hypnosis, or just isolated rumination. It is tempting to search for commonalities in all such practices, and no doubt social science will soon do so. MacIntyre (1981) provides a view of practice that makes this sort of approach possible.
5 For some specific examples and how they affect consciousness, see the collection of articles on transpersonal psychologies in Tart (1975), especially that by Chauduri.
6 Because I am using Wilber's scheme only in part and as a source of inspiration for my own thinking, the particular features of this level of transpersonal sensitivity

will not be detailed here. Wilber's general view that there are various stages or levels of religious consciousness provides moral support for my efforts here and helps make explicit my dissatisfaction with received social scientific efforts to understand the processes of joining a group with meditative practices as mere horizontal translation from one form of local knowledge to another.

7 Wolff even discusses Zen but in a way that is not very useful. His analysis is hindered by his assumption of the standard socialization model criticized previously in which a Zen practitioner is viewed as being resocialized into a traditional role (one Wolff calls "Zen craftsman"); his lack of first-hand experience in a Zen (or similar meditative) setting and with meditative practice; and his lack of information on the phenomenology of concentration as it exists in classic texts on meditation.

8 For a brief statement of a method of research based on a form of bracketing, see Jack Douglas's (1970) discussion of the "theoretic stance."

9 The materials in this section appeared previously in Preston, (1982).

10 See Chapter 7 in Shapiro (1980) for an excellent review of the relevant literature. Also see Akishige (1977) for a collection of Japanese psychological studies of Zen.

VII. Doing Zen Meditation

1 Tambiah offers a brief but helpful statement of the nature of self, cause, and illness in Buddhism contrasted with common assumptions of same in the West. Cf. "A Thai Cult of Healing Through Meditation," in Tambiah (1985, 87–122).

2 Sudnow's use of the term "normative" differs considerably in meaning from the more common usage that puts emphasis on the importance of rules and rational social actors implementing rules of action to account for social activity. It is just this latter view that Sudnow's work is used here to criticize.

3 See Cicourel (1970) for an alternative discussion of the basic rules of reality construction.

4 See Kiefer in White (1974) for an account of the difficulty that is introduced by attempting to self-observe to report on the meditative state.

5 The following discussion is indebted to Wilber (1979).

6 The presence of social pressure here might seem to contradict the point made in both Chapters V and VIII that Zen practice is characterized by much less intensive interaction and social pressure to conform than is usually found in settings where conversion occurs. The difference is that the pressure felt in the Zen setting is largely self-imposed. There is a well-known rule against moving while meditating, of course, but the sanctions are slight and rarely if ever administered in a way that publicly shames the offender. Some practitioners move without worrying about it (seemingly), although they are usually beginners or persons who are unable for whatever reasons to enter the meditative state successfully. The pressure I felt not to move reflected more my commitment to the practice and, more personally, to the teacher and those I might disturb by moving than any fear of regulation by the group. See Chapter VIII for further discussion of this point.

7 Dumoulin's (1963) view of some forms of Zen practice as "magical" efforts, in the pejorative sense, might well apply to my efforts at this point.

8   Mead discussed pain briefly and sees an escape from pain in shifting attention to something else (1934, 169).

9   Benson's claim that the consequences of meditation are understandable in terms of relaxation practices alone is rejected by Goleman (1977, xxiv), who argues that "the so-called 'relaxation response,' ... is simply another term for a normal physiological state.... This calm state is a pleasant experience, but it has little to do with the meditative states that transcend the normal limits of sensory awareness and that are the basis of religious mysticism."

10   Practitioners are theoretically predisposed to this experience because *sesshin,* a period of intensive practice, is usually defined as meaning "to unify the mind."

11   Cf. Lebra (1976) and von Duerckheim (1962) for the Japanese context. For a more magical and tantric treatment of this same spiritual center, see Luk (1973).

VIII. The Social Organization of Zen Meditative Ritual Practice and Its Consequences

1   Some materials in this chapter appeared previously in Preston (1982).

2   Notice that what we define here as Zen practice is centered in the relationship between Bourdieu's "structure" and "habitus." Bourdieu's use of the term "practice," which emphasizes the consequences of habitus (namely, particular social actions) is rather different. Thus, our meaning of habitus resembles to a degree MacIntyre's notion of "virtue" (1981, 75), although we find his separation of virtue from what he calls "internal goods" unnecessarily dualistic.

3   Wilber (1980, 93–9) argues that these meditation-related activities are based in a post-mental-egoic form of consciousness and "self."

4   Cf. von Duerckheim (1962) for a treatment of spiritual practice and its consequences in Japan that is similar to ours but without a sociological focus. For a discussion of a somewhat similar but more ethereal nature, see Blyth's (1962) treatment of art and Zen characteristics associated with art. For an effort to measure personality change as a result of participation in long-term Zen practice, see MacPhillamy (1986).

5   Turner (1977) emphasizes this latter point as characteristic of some kinds of ritual forms. Others tend to produce trance and states of dissociation.

6   For three very different yet very helpful discussions of the notion of self in the broader sense of the term, see Hardacre (1986), McDaniel (1980), and Turner (1976).

7   Whether he sees a self that seeks autonomy behind the social self or whether this is just a facet of American culture is not clear in Goffman's writings. For a discussion of the changing notion of self in Goffman's work, see Collins (1980).

8   Upon reading this section, a monk who has recently moved away from the center told me that in fact there was considerable "cheating" on the schedule by senior participants during *sesshin,* although not of a kind that was obvious to beginners (or, apparently, to the writer). He spoke of it in a way that suggested it was a demonstration of seniority and privilege rather than marginality to the group. This is no doubt to be expected because ritual participation implicitly symbolizes group membership and there are, as argued in Chapter IV, three or four different ways of being a member of this group.

9   This is certainly open to discussion and Goffman (1974) and Tart (1975) have both taken exception.

10   The following discussion is condensed from an earlier paper (Preston, 1982).

11   What I am describing here is similar to what Goffman (1961) has referred to as "euphoria" but with an important difference. Being involved in an activity so that one can spontaneously do the appropriate action is understood by Goffman as a process of unselfconsciously sustaining a definition of the situation and transformations of this definition.

To be at ease in a situation is to be properly subject to these rules, entranced by the meanings they generate and stabilize; to be ill at ease means that one is ungrasped by immediate reality and that one looses the grasp that others have on it. To be awkward or unkempt, to talk or move wrong, is to be a dangerous giant, a destroyer of worlds. As any psychotic and comic ought to know, any accurately improper move can poke through the thin sleeve of immediate reality. (Goffman, 1961, 80–1)

This is an insightful statement of how realities are maintained but there is a problem with it when applied to the Zen, especially the *sesshin* setting. The reality produced and maintained in this setting is not so easily destroyed as Goffman would have it. Rather than a "thin sleeve" of reality that is sustained by rules, ideas, and mutual beliefs, the reality generated and sustained by a mature community of Zen practitioners doing *sesshin* is solidly grounded in states of bodymind that are produced and sustained by long-standing, disciplined practice. Further, in contrast to Goffman's use of Sullivan's concept of "selective inattention," which involves an effortless dissociation from all other events (Goffman, 1961, 38), Zen practice encourages an experience of reality that is open to everything with nothing excluded. It is sometimes said that in the Zen tradition, the enlightened Mind is just ordinary mind. Thus, the comic's accurately improper move may well be perceived not as a breaching influence but as it is in a particularly situated context – perhaps even funny.

12   See Gordon (1981) for a helpful review of the sociological literature on emotion and sentiments.

13   This concern with spiritual energies is not incompatible with Collins's concern because most generally his argument is that particular kinds of group solidarity are grounded in particular kinds of emotional contagion generated and maintained in particular ritual forms.

14   See Sekida (1975) for a discussion of such energies.

IX. The Meanings of Zen Practice

1   See, for example, the cogent yet vastly different discussions of meaning in Collins (1975, 103–11) and MacIntyre (1981). A recent work using a framework very similar to MacIntyre's is Bellah, Madsen, Sullivan, Swidler & Tipton (1985).

2   On this last point see Wieder (1974) for the importance and subtlety of such reality-building practices, Brown (1977) and Shapiro & Walsh (1984) for different accounts of how such practices can be slowed and even stopped.

3 See his discussion for an excellent presentation of the details of the Tibetan Buddhist text and a consideration of the psychological literature that bears on these categories.

4 Wuthnow (1976), influenced by Bellah's symbolic realism, presents an exceptionally clear statement of this position regarding realities that include mystical experiences. Damrell (1977) deals with the meaning of mystical experience in this largely cognitive fashion as well but implicitly acknowledges the problems of doing so.

5 For a related discussion of this point, see Lyman (1978, 122–4).

6 Wilber (1981) draws attention to the possibilities for social solidarity that go beyond the common sociological notions of traditional–modern, mechanical–organic, status–contract, for example, by outlining the image of the social action found therein. A very different approach to understanding social solidarity is being developed by scholars studying subconscious synchronizing processes in social interaction. Cf. Gregory (1983); Zernbavel (1981).

7 One of the most helpful and informed approaches to the study of religion that is potentially effected by this suggestion is Geertz (1966).

8 Taken from a mimeographed copy of a talk given at the Zen Center Los Angeles by Jan Chozen Soulé 24 February 1984.

References

Aitken, Robert Chotan. 1976. Foreword to *On Zen Practice: II,* edited by
    Hakuyu Taizan Maezumi and Bernard Tetsugen Glassman, pp. xi–
    xiii. Los Angeles: Center Publications.
————. 1978. *Zen Wave: Basho's Haiku and Zen.* New York: Weatherhill.
————. 1984. *The Mind of Clover: Essays in Zen Buddhist Ethics.* San
    Francisco: North Point Press.
Akishige, Yoshiharu. 1977. *Psychological Studies in Zen: I and II.* Tokyo:
    Komazawa University.
Balch, Robert. 1980. "Looking Behind the Scenes in a Religious Cult:
    Implications for the Study of Conversion." *Sociological Analysis*
    41(2):137–43.
Balch, Robert, and Donald Taylor. 1977. "Seekers and Saucers: The Role
    of the Cultic Milieu in Joining a UFO Cult." *American Behavioral
    Scientist* 20(6):839–60.
Banquet, J. P. 1973. "Spectral Analysis of the EEG in Meditation."
    Electroencephalography and Clinical Neurophysiology 35:145–51.
Basabe, Fernando M., A. Shin, and F. Lanzaco. 1968. *Religious Attitudes
    of Japanese Men: A Sociological Survey.* Tokyo: Tuttle.
Becker, Howard S. 1953. "Becoming a Marijuana User." *American Journal
    of Sociology* 59(November):235–42.
Bellah, Robert N., Richard Madsen, W. J. Sullivan, Ann Swidler, and Steven
    Tipton. 1985. *Habits of the Heart: Individualism and Commitment
    in American Life.* Berkeley, Calif.: University of California Press.
Benedict, Ruth. 1946. *The Chrysanthemum and the Sword: Patterns of
    Japanese Culture.* New York: New American Library.
Benoit, Hubert. 1955. *The Supreme Doctrine: Psychological Studies in
    Zen Thought.* New York: The Viking Press.
Benson, Herbert. 1975. The Relaxation Response. New York: Morrow
    and Company.

Berger, Peter, and Thomas Luckmann. 1966. *The Social Construction of Reality.* Garden City, N.Y.: Doubleday.

Bird, Frederick. 1978. "Charisma and Ritual in New Religious Movements." In *Understanding the New Religions,* edited by J. Needleman and G. Baker, pp. 173–89. New York: Seabury Press.

Bittner, Egon. 1973. "Objectivity and Realism in Sociology." In *Phenomenological Sociology: Issues and Applications,* edited by G. Psathas, pp. 109–25. New York: John Wiley and Sons.

Blyth, R. H. 1962. *Zen and Zen Classics,* vol. 7. Tokyo: Hakuseido Press.

Bourdieu, Pierre. 1977. *Outline of a Theory of Practice.* Cambridge: Cambridge University Press.

Boyle, Richard P. 1985. "The Dark Side of Mead: The Structures of Mystical Teachings: Implications for Social Theory." In *Studies in Symbolic Interaction,* vol. 6, edited by Norman K. Denzin, pp. 59–78. Greenwich, Conn.: JAI Press.

Bromley, David G., and Anson D. Shupe, Jr. 1979. *"Moonies" in America: Cult, Church, and Crusade.* Beverly Hills, Calif.: Sage.

Brown, Daniel P. 1977. "A Model for the Levels of Concentrative Meditation." *International Journal of Clinical and Experimental Hypnosis* 25(4):236–73.

Bush, Diane M., and Roberta G. Simmons. 1981. "The Socialization of Sentiments and Emotion." In *Social Psychology: Sociological Perspectives,* edited by Morris Rosenberg and Ralph H. Turner, pp. 562–92. New York: Basic Books.

Campbell, Joseph. 1968. *The Hero with a Thousand Faces.* Princeton, N.J.: Princeton University Press.

Carrington, Patricia. 1977. *Freedom in Meditation.* Garden City, N.Y.: Doubleday.

Carroll, Jackson W., and David A. Roozen. 1979. "Continuity and Change: The Shape of Religious Life in the United States, 1950 to the Present." In *Religion in America: 1950 to the Present,* edited by J. W. Carroll, D. W. Johnson, and M. E. Marty, pp. 1–46. San Francisco: Harper and Row.

Cicourel, Aaron V. 1970. "Basic and Normative Rules in the Negotiation of Status and Role." In *Recent Sociology,* no. 2, edited by Hans Peter Dreitzel, pp. 4–45. New York: MacMillan.

Collins, Randall. 1975. *Conflict Sociology: Toward an Explanatory Science.* New York: Academic Press.

———. 1980. "Erving Goffman and the Development of Modern Social Theory." In *The View from Goffman,* edited by J. Ditton, pp. 170–209. New York: St. Martin's Press.

———. 1981. "On the Microfoundations of Macrosociology." *American Journal of Sociology* 6(5):984–1011.

Conway, Flo, and Jim Siegelman. 1978. *Snapping: America's Epidemic of Sudden Personality Change.* New York: Delta.

Coulter, Jeff. 1979. "Beliefs and Practical Understanding." In *Everyday Language: Studies in Ethnomethodology.* edited by G. Psathas, pp. 163–86. New York: Irvington Publishers.

Czikszentmihalyi, Mihalyi. 1975. *Beyond Boredom and Anxiety.* San Francisco: Jossey-Bass.

Damrell, Joseph. 1977. *Seeking Spiritual Meaning.* Beverly Hills, Calif.: Sage.

Deikman, Arthur J. 1966. "De-automatization and the Mystic Experience." *Psychiatry* 29(4):324–38.

Douglas, Jack, ed. 1970. *Understanding Everyday Life: Toward the Reconstruction of Sociological Knowledge.* Chicago: Aldine.

Dumoulin, Heinrich. 1963. *A History of Zen Buddhism.* New York: Pantheon.

Durkheim, Emile. 1965 (1915). *The Elementary Forms of the Religious Life,* translated by Joseph Ward Swain, Glencoe, Ill.: Free Press.

Eliade, Mircea. 1969. *Yoga: Immortality and Freedom.* Princeton, N.J.: Princeton University Press.

Ellwood, Robert. 1979. *Alternative Alters: Unconventional and Eastern Spirituality in America.* Chicago: University of Chicago Press.

———. 1980. *Mysticism and Religion.* Englewood Cliffs, N.J.: Prentice-Hall.

Fields, Rick. 1981. *How the Swans Came to the Lake: A Narrative History of Buddhism in America.* Boulder, Colo.: Shambhala.

Fingarette, Herbert. 1963. *The Self in Transformation.* New York: Basic Books.

Fontana, Andrea, and David van de Water. 1977. "The Existential Thought of Jean-Paul Sartre and Maurice Merleau-Ponty." In *Existential Sociology,* edited by Jack Douglas and John Johnson, pp. 101–29. Cambridge: Cambridge University Press.

Frank, Jerome D. 1961. *Persuasion and Healing: A Comparative Study of Psychotherapy.* Baltimore: Johns Hopkins University Press.

Frumkin, Kenneth, Robert J. Nathan, Maurice F. Prout, and Mariam C. Cohen. 1978. "Nonpharmacologic Control of Essential Hypertension in Man: A Critical Review of the Experimental Literature." *Psychosomatic Medicine.* 40(4):294–320.

Gallup, George, Jr. 1979. "Afterword: A Coming Religious Revival?" In *Religion in America: 1950 to the Present,* edited by J. W. Carroll, D. W. Johnson, and M. E. Marty, pp. 111–18. San Francisco: Harper and Row.

Gecas, Victor. 1981. "Contexts of Socialization." In *Social Psychology:*

Sociological Perspectives, edited by Morris Rosenberg and Ralph H. Turner, pp. 165–99. New York: Basic Books.

Geertz, Clifford. 1966. "Religion as a Cultural System." In *Anthropological Approaches to the Study of Religion,* edited by Michael Bonton, pp. 1–46. New York: Praeger.

Gergen, Kenneth. 1982. *Toward Transformation in Social Knowledge.* New York: Springer Verlag.

Gerlach, Luther, and Virginia Hine. 1970. *People, Power and Change.* Indianapolis: Bobbs-Merrill.

Glock, Charles Y., and Robert N. Bellah, eds. 1976 *The New Religious Consciousness.* Berkeley, Calif.: University of California Press.

Goffman, Erving. 1961. *Asylums.* Garden City, N.Y.: Doubleday.

———. 1967. "On Face Work: An Analysis of Ritual Elements in Social Interaction." In *Interaction Ritual: Essays on Face to Face Behavior.* New York: Doubleday.

———. 1974. *Frame Analysis: An Essay on the Organization of Experience.* New York: Harper and Row.

Goleman, Daniel. 1977. *The Varieties of the Meditative Experience.* New York: Dutton.

Gordon, David. 1974. "The Jesus People: An Identity Synthesis Interpretation." *Urban Life and Culture* 3(2):159–79.

———. 1984. "Dying to Self: Self-Control Through Self-Abandonment." *Sociological Analysis* 45(1):41–56.

Gordon, Steven L. 1981. "The Sociology of Sentiments and Emotion." In *Social Psychology: Sociological Perspectives,* edited by Morris Rosenberg and Ralph H. Turner, pp. 133–64. New York: Basic Books.

Gregory, Stanford W., Jr. 1983. "A Quantative Analysis of Temporal Symmetry in Microsocial Relations." *American Sociological Review* 48(February):129–35.

Hardacre, Helen. 1986. *Kurozumikyo and the New Religions of Japan.* Princeton, N.J.: Princeton University Press.

Harrison, Michael. 1974. "Preparation for Life in the Spirit: The Process of Initial Commitment to a Religious Movement." *Urban Life and Culture* 2:387–414.

Heirich, Max. 1977. "Change of Heart: A Test of Some Widely Held Theories about Religious Conversion." *American Journal of Sociology.* 83(3):653–80.

Hirai, Tomio. 1974. *Phychophysiology of Zen.* Tokyo: Igaku Shoin.

Hochschild, Arlie R. 1979. "Emotion Work, Feeling Rules, and Social Structure." *American Journal of Sociology* 85:551–75.

Izard, Carroll E. 1977. *Human Emotions.* New York: Plenum.

Izutzu, Toshihiko. 1982. *Toward a Philosophy of Zen Buddhism.* Boulder, Colo.: Prajna Press.

Jacobs, Janet. 1984. "The Economy of Love in Religious Commitment: The Deconversion of Women From Nontraditional Religious Movements." *Journal for The Scientific Study of Religion.* 23(2):155–71.

James, William. 1890. *Principles of Psychology.* New York: Holt.

———. 1961 (1902). *Varieties of the Religious Experience.* New York: Collier.

Johansson, Rune. 1969. *The Psychology of Nirvana.* London: Allen and Unwin.

Johnson, Willard. 1982. *Glossary of Technical Terms for the Academic Study of Religion.* La Jolla, Calif.: Ben-Sen Press.

Johnston, William. 1978. *The Inner Eye of Love: Mysticism and Religion.* San Francisco: Harper and Row.

Kapleau, Philip., ed. 1967. *The Three Pillars of Zen.* Boston: Reidel.

Kasulis, T. P. 1981. *Zen Action, Zen Person.* Honolulu: University Press of Hawaii.

Kiefer, Durand. 1974. "EEG Alpha Feedback and Subjective States of Consciousness: A Subject's Introspective Overview." In *Frontiers of Consciousness: The Meeting Ground Between Inner and Outer Reality,* edited by John White, pp. 94–113.

King, Winston L. 1980. *Theravada Meditation: The Buddhist Transformation of Yoga.* University Park, Pa.: The Pennsylvania State University Press.

Kotarba, Joseph A., and Andrea Fontana, eds. 1984. *The Existential Self in Society.* Chicago: University of Chicago Press.

Laing, R. D. 1967. *The Politics of Experience.* Edinburgh: Tavistock.

Lasch, Christopher. 1979. *The Culture of Narcissism.* New York: Norton.

Laski, Marghanita. 1961. *Ecstasy: A Study of Some Secular and Religious Experiences.* London: Cresset Press.

Lebra, Takie Sugiyama. 1976. Japanese Patterns of Behavior. Honolulu: University of Hawaii Press.

Leggett, Trevor. 1978. *Zen and the Ways.* Boston: Routledge and Kegan Paul.

Levine, Steven. 1982. *Who Dies? An Investigation of Conscious Living and Conscious Dying.* Garden City, N.Y.: Doubleday.

Lofland, John. 1966. *Doomsday cult.* Englewood Cliffs, N.J.: Prentice Hall.

———. 1977. "Becoming a World-Saver Revisited." *American Behavioral Scientist.* 20(6):805–19.

Lofland, John, and Rodney Stark. 1965. "Becoming a World-Saver." *American Sociological Review* 30:862–74.

Lofland, John, and Norman Skonovd. 1981. "Conversion Motifs." *Journal for the Scientific Study of Religion.* 20(4):373–85.

Long, Theodore, and Jeffery Hadden. 1983. "Religious Conversion and Socialization." *Journal for the Scientific Study of Religion.* 22(1):1– 14.

Luk, Charles, ed. 1973. *Taoist Yoga: Alchemy and Immortality.* New York: Weiser.

Lyman, Stanford. 1978. *The Seven Deadly Sins: Society and Evil.* New York: St. Martin's Press.

McDaniel, Jay. 1980. "Zen and the Self." *Process Studies* 10(3–4):110– 19.

McGuire, Meredith. 1981. *Religion: The Social Context.* Belmont, Calif.: Wadsworth.

MacIntyre, Alasdair. 1981. *After Virtue: A Study in Moral Theory.* Notre Dame: University of Notre Dame Press.

MacPhillamy, Douglas J. 1986. "Some Personality Effects of Long-Term Zen Monasticism and Religious Understanding." *Journal for the Scientific Study of Religion* 25(3):304–19.

Maliszewski, Michael, Stuart W. Twemlow, Daniel P. Brown, and John M. Engler. 1981. "A Phenomenological Typology of Intensive Meditation." *Revision* (Fall/Winter):3–27.

Manning, Peter K., and Horacio Fabrega, Jr. 1973. "The Experience of Self and Body: Health and Illness in the Chiapas Highlands." In *Phenomenological Sociology: Issues and Applications,* edited by G. Psathas, pp. 251–301. New York: John Wiley and Sons.

Mead, George H. 1934. *Mind, Self and Society,* edited by C. W. Morris. Chicago: University of Chicago Press.

Merleau-Ponty, Maurice. 1962. *Phenomenology of Perception.* New York: Humanities Press.

———. 1964. *Sense and Non-Sense.* Evanston, Ill.: Northwestern University Press.

———. 1968. *The Visible and the Invisible.* Evanston, Ill.: Northwestern University Press.

Merton, Thomas. 1968. *Zen and the Birds of Appetite.* New York: New Directions.

Messinger, Sheldon L., Harold Sampson, and Robert D. Towne. 1962. "Life as Theater: Some Notes on the Dramaturgic Approach to Social Reality." *Sociometry* 25:98–110.

Naranjo, Claudio, and Robert Ornstein. 1971. *On the Psychology of Meditation.* New York: Penguin Books.

Natanson, Maurice. 1970. *The Journeying Self: A Study in Philosophy and Social Role.* Reading, Mass.: Addison-Wesley.

Osis, Karlis, Edwin Bokert, and Mary Lou Carlson. 1973. "Dimensions of the Meditative Experience." *Journal of Transpersonal Psychology* 5(1):109–35.

Park, Sung Bae. 1983. *Buddhist Faith and Sudden Enlightenment.* Albany, N.Y.: State University of New York Press.

Polanyi, Michael. 1967. *The Tacit Dimension.* Garden City, N.Y.: Doubleday.

Pollner, Mel. 1979. "Explicative Transactions: Making and Managing Meaning in Traffic Court." In *Everyday Language: Studies in Ethnomethodology,* edited by G. Psathas, pp. 227–55. New York: Irvington Publishers.

Preston, David L. 1981. "Becoming a Zen Practitioner." *Sociological Analysis* 42(1):47–55.

———. 1982. "Meditative Ritual Practice and Spiritual Conversion-Commitment: Theoretical Implications Based on the Case of Zen." *Sociological Analysis* 43(3):257–70.

Robbins, Thomas, Dick Anthony, and James Richardson. 1978. "Theory and Research on Today's 'New Religions.' " *Sociological Analysis* 39(2):95–122.

Robbins, Thomas, and Dick Anthony, eds. 1981. *In Gods We Trust: New Patterns of Religious Pluralism in America.* New Brunswick, N.J.: Transaction Books.

Robinson, Richard H., and Willard L. Johnson. 1982. *The Buddhist Religion: A Historical Introduction.* Belmont, Calif.: Wadsworth.

Sansom, George B. 1978. *Japan: A Short Cultural History.* Palo Alto, Calif.: Stanford University Press.

Sargant, W. 1957. *Battle for the Mind.* New York: Doubleday.

Schutz, Alfred. 1967. *Collected Papers: I,* edited by Maurice Natanson. The Hague: Martinus Nijhoff.

Schwartz, Gary E., Richard J. Davidson, and Daniel J. Goleman. 1980. "Patterning of Cognitive and Somatic Processes in the Self-Regulation of Anxiety: Effects of Meditation vs. Exercise." *Psychosomatic Medicine* 40(June):321–8.

Sekida, Katsuki. 1975. *Zen Training: Methods and Philosophy.* New York: Weatherhill.

Shapiro, Deane H., Jr. 1980. *Meditation: Self-regulation Strategy and Altered State of Consciousness.* New York: Aldine.

Shapiro, Deane H., Jr., and Roger N. Walsh. 1984. *Meditation: Classical and Contemporary Perspectives.* New York: Aldine.

Stone, Donald. 1976. "The Human Potential Movement." In *The New Religious Consciousness,* edited by Charles Glock and Robert Bellah, pp. 93–115. Berkeley, Calif.: University of California Press.

———. 1978. "New Religious Consciousness and Personal Religious Experience." *Sociological Analysis* 39(2):123–34.

Straus, Roger. 1976. "Changing Oneself: Seekers and the Creative Transformation of Life Experience." In *Doing Social Life,* edited by John Lofland, pp. 252–72. New York: John Wiley and Sons.

———. 1979. "Religious Conversion as a Personal and Collective Accomplishment." *Sociological Analysis* 40(2):158–65.

———. 1981. "The Social-Psychology of Religious Experience: A Naturalistic Approach." *Sociological Analysis* 42(1):57–67.

Stryker, Sheldon. 1980. *Symbolic Interactionism: A Social Structural View.* Menlo Park, Calif.: Benjamin/Cummings.

Sudnow, David. 1978. *Ways of the Hand: The Organization of Improvised Conduct.* New York: Harper and Row.

———. 1979. *Talk's Body: A Meditation Between Two Keyboards.* New York: Penguin.

Suzuki, D. T. 1952. *Essays in Zen Buddhism* (2nd series). Boston: Beacon.

———. 1956. *Zen Buddhism: Selected writings of D. T. Suzuki,* edited by William Barrett, Garden City, N.Y.: Doubleday Anchor.

———. 1959. *Zen and Japanese Culture.* Princeton, N.J.: Princeton University Press. .

———. 1972. *Japanese Spirituality,* translated by Norman Waddell. Tokyo: Ministry of Education.

Tambiah, Stanley J. 1985. *Culture, Thought and Social Action: An Anthropological Approach.* Cambridge, Mass.: Harvard University Press.

Tart, Charles T., ed. 1969. *Altered States of Consciousness.* New York: John Wiley and Sons.

———, ed. 1975. *Transpersonal Psychologies.* New York: Harper and Row.

———. 1975a. *States of Consciousness.* New York: Dutton.

Thera, Nyanaponika. 1969. *The Heart of Buddhist Meditation.* New York: Citadel Press.

Tipton, Steven M. 1979. "New Religious Movements and the Problem of a Modern Ethic." *Sociological Inquiry* 49(2/3):286–313.

———. 1982. *Getting Saved from the Sixties: Meaning in Conversion and Cultural Change.* Berkeley, Calif.: University of California Press.

Tiryakian, Edward A. 1968. "The Existential Self and the Person." In *The Self in Social Interaction* I, edited by Chad Gordon and Kenneth J. Gergen, pp. 75–86. New York: John Wiley and Sons.

Trungpa, Chogyam. 1973. *Cutting Through Spiritual Materialism,* edited by John Baker and Glen Eddy. Berkeley, Calif.: Shambhala.

Turner, Ralph H. 1976. "The Real Self: From Institution to Impulse." *American Journal of Sociology* 18(March):989–1016.

Turner, Victor. 1977. "Variations on a Theme of Liminality." In *Secular Ritual,* edited by Sally F. Moore and Barbara G. Myerhoff, pp. 36–52. Amsterdam: Van Gorcum.

von Duerckheim, Karlfried. 1977 (1962). *Hara: The Vital Centre of Man,* translated by Sylvia-Monica Kospoth. London: Unwin.

Wagner, Helmut. 1973. "The Scope of Phenomenological Sociology:

Considerations and Suggestions." In *Phenomenological Sociology: Issues and Applications*, edited by G. Psathas, pp. 61–87. New York: John Wiley and Sons.

Wallace, Robert Keith, Herbert Benson, and Archie F. Wilson. 1971. "A Wakeful Hypometabolic Physiologic State." *American Journal of Physiology* 221:795–9.

Wieder, D. Lawrence. 1974. *Language and Social Reality*. The Hague: Martinus Nijhoff.

Wilber, Ken. 1977. *The Spectrum of Consciousness*. Wheaton, Ill.: Theosophical Publishing.

———. 1979. *No Boundary: Eastern and Western Approaches to Personal Growth*. Los Angeles: Center Publications.

———. 1980. *The Atman Project: A Transpersonal View of Human Development*. Wheaton, Ill.: Theosophical Publishing.

———. 1981. *Up From Eden: A Transpersonal View of Human Evolution*. Garden City, N.Y.: Doubleday.

———. 1983. *A Sociable God: A Brief Introduction to a Transcendental Sociology*. New York: McGraw-Hill.

Wilson, Steven. 1984. "Becoming a Yogi: Resocialization and Deconditioning as Conversion Processes." *Sociological Analysis* 45(4):301–14.

Wilson, Thomas P. 1970. "Normative and Interpretive Paradigms." In *Understanding Everyday Life: Toward the Reconstruction of Sociological Knowledge*, edited by Jack Douglas, pp. 57–79. Chicago: Aldine.

Wolff, Kurt. 1976. *Surrender and Catch: Experience and Inquiry Today*. Boston: Reidel.

Wuthnow, Robert. 1976. "The New Religions in Social Context." In *The New Religious Consciousness*, edited by Charles Glock and Robert Bellah, pp. 267–93. Berkeley, Calif.: University of California Press.

———. 1976a. *The Consciousness Reformation*. Berkeley, Calif.: University of California Press.

Yamada, Koun. 1979. *Gateless Gate*. Los Angeles: Center Publications.

Yasutani, Hakuun. 1967. "The Lectures." In *The Three Pillars of Zen*, edited by Philip Kapleau, pp. 26–62. Boston: Beacon.

———. 1973. "Commentary on Bodhidharma's Emptiness." *ZCLA Journal*. Summer/Fall: 19–24.

Zaner, Richard M. 1964. *The Problem of Embodiment: Some Contributions to a Phenomenology of the Body*. The Hague: Martinus Nijhoff.

———. 1981. *The Context of Self: A Phenomenological Inquiry Using Medicine as a Clue*. Athens, Oh.: Ohio University Press.

Zernbavel, Eviator. 1981. *Hidden Rhythms*. Chicago: University of Chicago Press.

Index

169